THE
GENESIS
PRINCIPLE
FOR
PARENTS

THE GENESIS PRINCIPLE FOR PARENTS

Pat Hershey Owen

 Tyndale House
Publishers, Inc.
Wheaton, Illinois

Dedicated to my husband
BOB OWEN
whose skilled editing
and writing assistance
has created the cooperative ambience
in which this book was written
and whose godly living
in every dimension of life
has created the blessed ambience
in which this book is lived

Unless otherwise noted, all Scripture quotations
are taken from the King James (Authorized)
Version.

First printing, September 1985
Library of Congress Catalog Card Number 85-50673
ISBN 0-8423-0996-9
Copyright © 1985 by Pat Hershey Owen
Printed in the United States of America

CONTENTS

CONTENTS

1: SOWING TOMORROW'S HARVEST

It had been a long day. I propped myself comfortably in my chair, adjusted the light, and opened my Bible. I began reading these words in Galatians 6:7, "Be not deceived; God is not mocked: for whatsoever a man soweth, that shall he also reap"—*that shall he also reap . . . that shall he also reap. . . .*

And while I was meditating on this thought, I fell asleep.

In a dream, I was sitting in the semidarkness of my church's sanctuary. Only a soft light filled the room. I looked about me and, at first, saw no one.

As it always is, the gentle ambience of my church was restful. I settled back in my seat to enjoy the solitude. But as I did so, I became aware that I was not alone.

I heard no sound, but felt certain of another presence. As I turned, I saw a gentleman walking down the aisle—a man I immediately recognized as Mr. Reader, a member of our congregation.

As usual, Mr. Reader carried a book under his arm. My eyes followed him as he silently moved down the aisle.

Suddenly, the thought hit me with force: How much Mr. Reader's children resembled him! They always had books under their arms. And I knew the oldest son was a very fine professor.

I looked for Mr. Reader again, but he was nowhere to be seen. Before I had time to muse on the meaning of his appearance, I sensed again that I was not alone. This time as I turned, I saw Mr. Bonds. He made his way down the aisle, looking neither right nor left, but straight ahead. His little boy followed close behind him.

Mr. Bonds tightly clasped a bag in his two hands, as did his son. Somehow I knew those bags were full of money. I also knew, as did most of the congregation, that Mr. Bonds treated his wife miserably. I wondered why God had blessed him financially.

Even as this question attached itself in my mind, I saw Mr. Bonds and the boy move wraithlike down the aisle. Then they, too, were gone.

As in a procession, Marty Ritus came next, hobbling painfully down the aisle. She carried a basket brimming with the sugar cookies she baked for her children to give to the neighbors. Marty loved the Lord and was always preparing rich desserts for others. Why then, I thought, does God allow her and her children to be sick so frequently?

By now I anticipated another arrival. I had only moments to wait. Mr. Workman strode in, newspaper and *Time* magazine in one hand, attaché case in the other. In half the time it took the others, Mr. Workman had hurried down the aisle.

But abruptly he stopped and turned, looking back. He spoke, and his voice seemed to echo as though he spoke into a rain barrel.

"Children! Children! Where are you? Where . . . ? Where . . . ?" The haunting word echoed and reechoed, gradually diminishing till it was gone.

Doesn't he realize, I wondered, that his wayward children left home years ago?

It was then that I felt my husband gently shaking me. "You must have been dreaming," he said. "You had such a puzzled look on your face."

"Yes, I must have been dreaming," I repeated, remembering the strange sights I had witnessed. I arose and prepared for bed, only to lie awake for a long time pondering the meaning of my unusual dream.

And when the morning broke, shining bright rays through my priscilla curtains and onto my face, the dream flooded back to me. Again I pondered its meaning. But soon the day's activities crowded it out of my thoughts.

Breakfast dishes washed, dried, and put away, I donned my wide-brimmed hat and gloves. For the next hour, I weeded and watered my flower garden. As the sun ascended higher, I wiped perspiration from my brow and surveyed my work. It was lovely.

Sweet peas eagerly climbed their trellises, profusely covered with fragrant blossoms. My roses, each of them a champion, had exceeded my expectations. My zinnias, knee-high, bowed low with buds. Pansies, fuchsias, gardenias, and more—all of them so very responsive to my efforts on their behalf.

My garden was my joy. I could always count on an abundant harvest when I had done my part. Our home was fragrant with the fruits of my toil. Already I had cut and arranged bright bunches of daisies for my breakfast table.

Then it came to me: the meaning of my dream!

Full-blown. In detail.

I rushed to my desk and grabbed my pencil and paper.

At the top of the page, I wrote three words: God's Genesis Principle. Everything I had done in my garden this morning, everything I had dreamed last night, involved the same God-given principle of sowing and reaping.

In the Book of Genesis, God did more than create the heavens and the earth, the animals, and Adam and Eve. He also set in motion an irrevocable law that I'll call the Genesis Principle. This law stipulates that everything is to bring forth fruit abundantly after its kind. That means plants and animals. That means people.

"And he said, 'Let the earth burst forth with every sort of grass and seed-bearing plant, and fruit trees with seeds inside the fruit, so that these seeds will produce the kinds of plants and fruits they came from.' And so it was, and God was pleased" (Gen. 1:11, 12, TLB).

God also said, " 'Let the earth bring forth the living creature according to its kind: cattle and creeping thing and beast of the earth, each according to its kind. . . .' And God saw that it was good" (Gen. 1:24, 25, NKJV).

My pencil was moving faster and faster.

In my garden, I had sown and tended flower seeds. And now I was rewarded with row after row, bush after bush, trellis after trellis of flowers—each one reproduced after its own kind.

My dream also had to do with the sowing and reaping process. Each person in my dream had planted seeds in his childrens' lives. And what I had witnessed were the fruits.

By now my pencil was much too slow for the

thoughts rushing into my head. I was aware that God was showing me something special, something I must learn, something all parents should learn. I turned to my typewriter and began to write. . . .

2: SOWING GOD'S WAY

"Ross!" Barbara called. "Come quickly!"

Five-year-old Ross clambered down the basement stairs and hurried to the corner where his mother was bending over a box. "What do you want, Mother?" he asked breathlessly.

Barbara pointed to the box. "Look, Dusty's kittens have come."

Ross surveyed the kittens momentarily, then without a word turned and ran back up the stairs. A minute later he was back with a picture in his hand. He stood looking in the box, glancing first at his picture, then at Dusty and her tiny kittens.

"What's the matter, Ross?" Barbara asked, hearing her son's sigh.

"I wanted a kitten like my picture," he said slowly. "And not one of them's orange and black and white like my picture."

"But they're such pretty little kittens," Barbara said.

Ross sighed again. "Well, they're OK. But I wanted a calico kitten . . . and these are all gray." He looked up into his mother's face, a puzzled look in his eyes. "Why are they all gray, Mother? Why aren't there any ones like my picture?"

Barbara put her arm around her small son's shoulders. "Because both the mother and the daddy cats were gray."

"But couldn't they have had just *one* calico kitten? Just one?"

Barbara shook her head. "No, Ross. Dusty's kittens look just like her and the daddy."

Comprehension began to dawn in the boy's eyes. "You mean, if the daddy had looked like my picture, then some of the kittens would have looked like him?"

Barbara smiled. "That's right, son. That's God's Genesis Principle."

"OK, stand right there," the photographer said. "Now, Miss Aimes, smile. There, I've got it."

Sandra's smile faded as she once again ran her eyes over her lovely display of tomatoes at the county fair—a display prominently decorated with a huge blue ribbon. For the third year in a row, she'd won first prize for her carefully cultivated tomatoes.

"Aren't you pleased?" her friend Kimberly asked.

"Yes . . . ," Sandra said slowly, "I'm very pleased. Except that. . . ."

"Except what?" Kimberly asked. "You've done it again—produced the best tomatoes in the county. Except what?"

"Well, my tomatoes *are* lovely, but I don't seem to have any success with anything else. And . . . ," she looked wistfully at the display next to hers, "Alec always gets first prize for his 'Garden Variety.' And," she went on, "you can't make a very good tossed salad with *just* tomatoes."

"Then why don't you grow something else?" Kimberly asked impatiently.

"Because I've spent all my time learning how to grow tomatoes."

Kimberly shrugged. "Well, you're reaping what you've sowed. You just can't change God's Genesis Principle."

It's easy to see how the Genesis Principle works in nature, but it's crucial to discern it at work in our family life as well.

As Christians we sometin.es make the mistake of relegating God's natural laws to a nonspiritual and thus unimportant place in our lives. But these laws were created for our benefit, and when we knowledge-ably walk in them, we prosper.

The laws of flight, for example, have existed since the moment of creation. But not until men unlocked the mysteries of aeronautics could they shake the dust of the earth from their feet.

Even then, the Wright brothers rose only a few feet from the earth during those first flights. As they came to understand the laws of flight better, they rose higher and higher. Today there's virtually no limit to the outer ranges of flight because people have learned and cooperated with God's principles.

In my spiritual struggles, I gradually began to see that in the same way God's Genesis Principle affects the growth of plants, it also affects every dimension of life—including parenting. And when we cooperate with this principle, we will reap a harvest of success.

Let's explore some of the ways God's natural law of sowing affects our roles as parents.

WE CHOOSE OUR SEEDS

Mr. Glen groaned as he slid his bulk out of the leather lounger in his den and waddled to the kitchen refrigerator. He opened it and slid out some cold cuts, bread, mayonnaise, and milk. He was in the middle of making himself a huge sandwich when his teenage son came in.

"Hi, Dad."

Mr. Glen looked up from his culinary creation. "Oh, hi, Ray. How did the game go tonight?"

"We lost."

"You lost?" Ray's father paused in his sandwich making. "You *lost?* But this was the play-off. You should have won!"

"Yeah," Ray answered indolently. He picked up a cold chicken breast and stuffed half of it in his mouth. With his mouth full of food he mumbled, "We should have won, I guess. But I messed up a couple of shots."

Mr. Glen put down his knife. "*You* blew a couple of shots? How'd that happen?"

Ray shrugged. "Just wasn't fast enough. The guy who was guarding me was just a little guy, but he outfoxed me. . . ."

The father ran his eyes over his teenage son. "No wonder you've slowed down. You gained a dozen pounds over the Thanksgiving holiday." He picked up his sandwich and poised for a bite. "You've got to watch your eating if you're going to be a ball player."

The boy paused, another bite of chicken and bread halfway to his mouth. Without a word, he resentfully surveyed his father's bulk.

Hal Thomas slipped into his jacket and rose wearily from the kitchen table. "Well, Mary, I'm off. Don't bother to wait up. See you in the morning."

"I wish you didn't have to go to work tonight," his wife said. "You look very tired."

"Yeah, Dad," Bert chimed in, "I wish you'd go to the concert with me tonight instead. I'm the choir's new soloist. And you haven't heard us sing even once."

Hal slapped his son affectionately on the shoulder. "Well, I took this second job to pay for that new car we all want."

His wife sighed deeply. "Bert so much wants you to hear him sing. . . ."

Hal checked his watch. "Well, we've gone over this before. I've got to go. Just another year and I'll be the most dedicated father at the concerts, Bert."

Addie roughly jerked her small child out of the playpen. "You cry *all* the time!" she shouted in the frightened child's face. "All the time! And I can't stand it!" She shook the baby, which caused him to wail even louder.

The outside door opened and two preschool boys ran in, leaving the door open. Addie shouted, "Somebody *close that door!* Hear me? Close the door!" Neither child listened, but ran through the house and out the back door, leaving both front and back doors open.

Addie started to shout again, but the child in her arms suddenly stiffened, arched his back, and stopped breathing. Terrified, Addie held the baby at arm's length and began crying.

"Oh, God, what do I do now?"

Meanwhile, the seizure ran its course and the baby hung limp as a doll in his mother's arms. Addie sat on the debris-littered divan in her messy living room and rocked the baby back and forth. The unconscious child was unaware of his mother's tears.

Every parent—every person, in fact—sows *some kind* of seeds. And whether our seeds are consciously or unconsciously sown makes little difference, because each of them will reproduce according to God's Genesis Principle. Seeds of a bad habit, seeds of neglect, seeds of stress—all will produce a corresponding harvest.

Have you ever said or heard, "Yes, my child is growing like a weed"?

How does a weed grow? Without restraint, with no prompting, with no cultivation or expectations. Does this comparison reflect our careless thinking concerning our children's growth?

Every parent must develop a sowing mentality, a realization that literally everything he does or says is a seed of some kind, sown in some soil. As a parent, as a human being, I must continually be aware of the kinds of seeds I am sowing. Not until I am conscious of my actions will I be able to plant seeds that will positively benefit myself, my family, and God's Kingdom. We cannot choose whether or not to plant. We can only choose our seeds.

WE PREPARE THE SOIL

My family and I once lived in a house where we noticed a considerable difference between the front and back lawns. The front lawn was beautiful, while the backyard remained sparse, uneven, and sickly, even though we cared for both of them the same way.

A neighbor watched me laboring in the front yard one day and commented on how nice it looked. "Yes," I said, "but you should see the backyard."

The neighbor nodded his head knowingly. "The previous owners spent a lot of time and money on this front yard. You know, they rototilled, fertilized, and planted it—really watched over it with tender loving care."

"And the backyard?"

He shook his head. "They didn't do anything but water it occasionally."

As they moved their trays along the school cafeteria line, the two teachers chatted about their respective classes. Betty Ralston, a first-year teacher, was puzzled about some of her children.

"Why is it," she asked Helen Halskel, a teacher of many years, "that some children catch on so quickly, while others are so slow to comprehend?"

"Betty, I puzzled over that very question for several years. But I think I have the answer."

They carried their trays to a quiet corner and sat down. "I used to believe it had something to do with the child's ability to adjust to school," Helen said. "But not anymore. Now I think it has to do with the early home environment."

"Do you mean the way the children get along with their parents and siblings?" Betty asked.

"Not entirely. I really think it has to do with the amount of time and effort the parents exercise in preparing the child to conceptualize, to think creatively, to be aware of the world around him. All of this early training gives a child the self-confidence that enables him to quickly respond to his teachers."

Betty nodded understandingly. "Yes, I see. That means the soil of his learning capabilities, so to speak, has already been tilled and prepared for a crop to be planted."

Helen smiled. "That's a good analogy."

Alison stayed behind after the others had left our Bible study. She said to me, "I want to talk with you."

"Let's have a cup of herbal tea," I said. "The water's hot."

Alison agreed. Moments later, we were seated on the

kitchen stools sipping the aromatic peppermint tea. I waited for her to speak. The question wasn't long in coming.

"Why is it," Alison said, setting her cup down, "that Genevieve is doing so well spiritually—she's, well, *victorious*—and I seem to struggle all the time?" She sighed. "We both dedicated our lives to the Lord the same night. I just don't understand what's wrong with me."

"I think I can relieve your mind," I said. "I know Genevieve about as well as I know you, and there's a significant difference in your backgrounds—a difference that accounts for the seeming disparity in your Christian lives."

Alison leaned toward me. "What is it? I must know."

"Well, you told me you had had absolutely no Christian background or teaching previous to this Bible study. Isn't that right?"

She nodded.

"But Genevieve did," I said. "When she was a little girl, she went to Sunday school regularly. She learned some principles that became a part of her. And though she hadn't made God the Lord of her life, still his Word was sown in her spirit. Now that she's an adult and exposed to Bible teaching again, her earlier roots in the Word have begun to grow quickly."

Alison contemplatively sipped her tea, then set her cup down. "I see. Genevieve had a foundation—the roots of her early preparation—to build on. I didn't. So nothing's wrong with me. I just can't grow as fast as she can until my roots become strong."

"That's it exactly."

As we nurture our children, we need to recognize that we are not only planting seeds, but also preparing the "soil" of their lives for future plantings. When we allow

a certain aspect of their lives to go untended, we
slow its later development

My husband has learned that when a person fails to
eat foods with certain vitamins and minerals, his body
tissues become depleted of those life-sustaining elements. At that point, it requires more than a maintenance dosage of the proper vitamins to bring the body
tissues back to health. Usually, this dosage exceeds
the basic maintenance level of vitamins by ten, twenty,
even fifty times.

In the same way, a person who allows himself to
become depleted spiritually must expose himself to
many times the usual or "maintenance amount" of
scriptural input, just to bring himself up to normal.
And not until he has literally saturated himself in the
Word of God over a longer period of time will God's
promises manifest themselves in his life to the same
degree he sees them being manifested in those who
have not gone through long periods of spiritual defi-
ciency.

Are we depleting—or nourishing—our children's
spirits, minds, and emotions?

We are preparing their "soil" for future plantings.

WE SOW SEEDS DAILY

Tommy and Eddy were next-door neighbors, and as
young teenagers they longed for the day when they
would be able to drive. Until that great day came,
though, they availed themselves of every possible
opportunity to be around their parents' cars.

One summer day, Tommy said, "Eddy, I've got an
idea. Let's wax cars today."

Eddy said, "I don't know how. I've never done it
before."

Tommy said, "I'll show you. I've done it lots of times."

So they assembled their paraphernalia and began to work on Tommy's father's car. Since it had been waxed frequently, it was soon shining brightly in the midsummer sun. Then the boys moved on to Eddy's dad's car.

They started in. They waxed and rubbed, rubbed and waxed. Two hours later, when they still hadn't finished the second car, Tommy paused. "This is really a big job."

"Yeah," Eddy said, wiping sweat from his face. "Your car was sure easier than mine."

Tommy nodded wisely. "Yes, it was," he said. "And it's all because my car had been waxed many times before."

Sara and Jan became involved in the Navigator's Scripture memorization plan. At the outset, Sara, who had been memorizing poems and Scriptures from childhood, found it easy to learn several verses within a few days. But it often took Jan several weeks to memorize a single verse. Nevertheless, despite the difficulty involved, Jan stuck with it. She doggedly learned her verses, little by little, one by one.

Finally one day, a couple of years later, Jan realized that she could memorize her verses more easily. In fact, she was now learning several verses a week.

Though Jan didn't know it at the time, her method of learning had been described long ago by the prophet Isaiah when he said, "For precept must be upon precept, precept upon precept; line upon line, line upon line; here a little, and there a little" (Isa. 28:10).

All sowing and reaping of scriptural and life principles occur in this way. The seed-sowing in our children's lives is done little by little, but the cumulative effect will one day result in an abundant harvest. When you daily sow positive seeds, you will receive a positive harvest in *every area* in which you have *continuously planted.*

We reap eventually when we sow continuously.

WE CAN PLANT AGAIN

Ben looked out the window at the garden. It looked different than it did last summer, but he wasn't at first sure why. He saw some large, vine-like plants spreading across the garden. They were *something* like the ones they had grown last year. But there seemed to be a difference.

"Mother," Ben asked, turning, "are those pumpkins growing in our garden?"

"No, Ben," she said, "they're watermelons."

"Watermelons?" Ben said in astonishment. "Where are the pumpkins?"

"We aren't having pumpkins this year."

"Why not?"

"Because we planted watermelons."

Ben looked disappointed. "But I wanted pumpkins. And now I can't ever have pumpkins." He started to cry.

Mary wiped away her small son's tears. "Yes, you can, Ben. If you like pumpkins, we'll plant them for you next year. Because each time you plant, you can grow a new harvest."

It was high noon. The campus clock authoritatively announced that fact to the college students who hurried past, each one bent on reaching his lunch or his next class.

My attention, however, was not upon these passersby, but upon the eager-faced young people who were clustered around my son Keith. He had just finished preaching the Word to this Bible study group and was fielding their questions. I turned toward my youngest son, David, who wore a pleased look on his face. David had taught this group each week for a whole school year, and today he was proud to share with them his older brother, who was preparing to leave on a missionary trip.

A prayer of thanksgiving flowed from my heart for the fact that *all three* of my sons were involved in ministry. (Terry, my oldest, was then pastor of the singles ministries at the Crystal Cathedral in Garden Grove, California.) Yet at one time, I would have doubted that David would ever join his older brothers in the Lord's service.

When David was younger and needed the attentive care of his parents, I was busily involved in my profession, seeking the world's standards of success. As a result, I sowed the seeds of neglect in my youngest son's life. A few years later, I finally grew aware that David, too, was busily looking for what the world could offer him—a direct consequence of my wrong seed-sowing.

As I saw the life David was living, I could see the harvest of my seeds, and I didn't like what I saw. So I began sowing another kind of seed: I spent much sacrificial time in prayer for this son.

Today, some years later, David is teaching the Word of God, and reaping a bountiful harvest for the Lord. The new seed I sowed produced a different kind of harvest.

Your *present harvest* is the result of a *previous sowing*. If you don't want to repeat today's harvest, you can do something about it: change your seeds. This is as true of the seed you are planting in your child's life as it is about the seed you plant in your garden.

This book deals with some specific ways to apply the principles of reaping and sowing in your life. Good health, a positive self-image, productive stewardship—

these and other qualities can develop in your children as you practice the Genesis Principle.

Personally, I have spent months, even years, learning how to live by the Genesis Principle in some of these areas. Sometimes I grew weary and discouraged, and sometimes I wanted to give up and quit.

Then one day I heard these encouraging words. God was speaking directly to me: "And let us not be weary in well-doing: for *in due season* we shall reap, if we faint not" (Gal. 6:9, emphasis added).

The *we* in that verse applied to me as well as to you—and to anyone who desires to apply the irrevocable Genesis Principle of sowing and reaping.

Some of you will say or think, "But, it's too late! My children are nearly grown," or, "The damage is already done."

But, my friend, *it's never too late.*

We will reap a new harvest when we plant new seeds.

3: HOW
TO REAP
RIGHTEOUSNESS

Roy is a farmer who raises a specially developed type of small, tough-skinned field tomato that can be harvested by machine. One summer as he was irrigating and cultivating his crop, he noticed that a considerable amount of the new growth consisted of larger than average tomatoes.

Roy was concerned and called the seed dealer. "Come out and look at my crop."

"Why?" the dealer asked.

"Come and see...."

When the dealer came, Roy pointed out the large tomatoes. "Where did they come from?" he asked.

The dealer examined the fruit. He shook his head.

"Roy, I don't know what to say. Somehow the hybrid seed I sold you got mixed with beefsteak tomato seed."

"I can see that," Roy said. "And now the crop is ruined. These beefsteak tomatoes can't be machine-harvested. It's going to cost more to harvest these tomatoes by hand than I'll receive from selling them."

For a number of years, my uncle grew and marketed oranges from his own groves. He didn't understand why some of his trees produced better oranges than others. Not until he learned the "secrets" of pollination did he realize that his poor crops were the result of cross-pollination with inferior trees.

Today most farmers know that selective breeding in cattle and careful pollination of plants are the secrets of better stock and fruits. Scientists have found that breeding a select and strong animal with another produces a superior stock, which means better beef and more milk in cattle, and better wool in sheep. In the same way, the selective growth of a pure strain of a fruit or a vegetable results in better produce.

Though scientists discovered the principles of cross-pollination fairly recently, God has known all about the subject from the beginning of his Creation. He told his people, "Thou shalt not sow thy vineyard with divers seeds: lest the fruit of thy seed which thou hast sown, and the fruit of thy vineyard, be defiled" (Deut. 22:9). And in the Book of Leviticus he said, "Thou shalt not let thy cattle gender with a diverse kind: thou shalt not sow thy field with mingled seed" (Lev. 19:19).

These Scriptures are important, not only for their scientific implications, but also for their spiritual applications. For example, God strongly warned his people that intermarriage with other tribal groups would cause the breakdown of religious and cultural standards. When these warnings were ignored, serious spiritual and social problems resulted.

We see another application in Luke 8. There the Word of God is likened to a seed. When this seed is planted with thorns—another kind of seed—it dies (Luke 8:11). God clearly commands us not to mix his Word with diverse seeds.

Could it be that our failure to heed this Scripture is the primary cause of poor spiritual harvests in our children? To reap a bigger, stronger, better, godly harvest in the lives of our children, we must sow the seed of God *according to his laws of sowing.*

PLANTING PURE SEEDS

How can we do this? What is the key to cultivating true godliness in our children?

The quality and amount of godly seeds you plant in your child's life are determined by your relationship with God. God says that if you do not obey his Word, "ye shall sow your seed in vain" (Lev. 26:16). But the parent who consistently, continuously sows obedience to God will reap a rich harvest of righteous living in his children and his children's children.

A godly parent plants the seeds of righteousness not only by his words, but also by his actions. His entire life is a sermon preached to his child. It speaks louder than any principles he can explain. It outlasts the performance of an hour here and there; it is the outflow of a well-fed walk with God.

Neither church services nor words of instruction have the power to impart life-giving truth to a child without being backed by a parent's righteous life. Few children will rise above the examples they see portrayed by their parents.

Unless a parent sows God's Word into his child by his very character and conduct, he will be sowing mixed, mingled, or even adulterated seeds.

The purpose of this chapter is not to advocate one

theological point of view, but to describe the spiritual "nutrients" that will equip you and your child for future growth in the Lord and help prevent possible cross-pollination by the sowing of negative seeds. These spiritual nutrients are prayer and God's Word.

PRAYER

Prayer, especially prayer for our families, is a serious matter, for the character of our prayer life will determine the character of our parenting. Only parents who make prayer a mighty force in their lives are powerful enough to advance God's cause in their family.

Talking to your children about God is important, but talking to God about your children is even more important. Parents who are effective in their prayer closets with God will be effective out in the open with their children. But if you have not learned how to talk to God about your children, you will never talk with real, lasting success to your children about God.

The superficial results of many a Christian home are rooted in the lack of prayer. Your home may evidence the signs of material success—a comfortable life, fame, or highly developed skills. But unless prayer is an evident and controlling force, there will be no spiritual success.

God's most successful parents are always distinguished by this one trait: they are people of prayer. Though they may differ in theology, these parents all pray so as to affect their own lives and the lives of their families. And their influence affects their world.

What Is Prayer? I'm not going to make any attempt to try to tell you how to pray, for many godly people have already written excellent books on the subject. But I will say this: One who prays develops an intimate relationship with his God. And intimate relationships are neither made nor maintained in a hurry.

My husband has become good friends with a Jewish rabbi who recently accepted the Messiahship of Jesus. A few days ago, my husband and a couple of friends were talking with the rabbi. One man asked him, "So now you believe in Jesus?"

The rabbi instantly responded, "Of course, I *believe* in him. But that's not most important. Millions of people believe in Jesus, but that belief has not changed their lives. The difference is, I *know* him. And we have a vital, intimate relationship."

That's the secret of effective prayer: knowing God and knowing God's Son. And developing that knowledge does not come about by accident. It comes through paying attention to his Word and spending much time with him alone.

According to the psalmist, prayer also involves praise. In fact, he says, praise is the proper method of approaching the throne of God. "Enter into his gates with thanksgiving, and into his courts with praise" (Ps. 100:4).

When the Israelites went to battle, the praisers were sent first, ahead of the fighters. Praise can promote victory in every dimension of our lives. God is present in praise. He inhabits the praises of his people (Ps. 22:3).

In my book *Seven Styles of Parenting,* a whole chapter is devoted to praise because of its tremendous importance in every home. Among its many benefits, praise sows seeds of gratitude.

Prayer involves a constant dialogue with God. The several months I worked at a Hebrew school provided me with both blessing and spiritual insight. There I met Adina, one of the school's beloved teachers. She taught the children to speak to God about *everything*— everything they saw, everything they thought.

For example, when they looked out the window and saw a lovely tree, she encouraged them to thank God, right at that moment, for the tree he had made. As they opened their books, she told them to thank God for eyes to see and a mind to understand the lesson. When someone gave them a gift or a treat, she trained them to thank God as well as the human giver.

Adina taught the children not only to thank God, but to do so aloud. She believed, as I do, that parents of very young children have marvelous opportunities to encourage this because every child likes to talk to someone, even if he has to make up his companion. Praying aloud to God can become a natural experience when it's introduced to children at an early age.

Adina probably taught the children as much through her example as through her instruction. If a child misbehaved, Adina would say aloud, "God, help me to be patient, and help Miriam to know that I love her and want to help her to learn."

I saw Adina's teaching take root. One day on the playground, I saw a boy strike a girl and take away her ball. The girl immediately responded, "God, forgive Daniel, and help me to show him that I want to be his friend."

Hearing the voice of God is the other part of our dialogue with him. God may put the names of others upon our minds for the purpose of praying for them— or doing something for them. We can develop the sensitivity to hear his voice by soaking ourselves in his Word, which is his written voice, and spending time in his presence.

When our lives are crammed with busy schedules, frenetic activity, excessive talking, and loud music, God's still, small voice is crowded out.

We need to take time to be quiet before the Lord, making listening time an integral part of our praying time.

Hindrances to Prayer. Many people say, "I find it difficult to pray."

One reason for this difficulty is that we sometimes harbor ill feelings and an unforgiving spirit. Jesus said, "And whenever you stand praying, forgive, if you have anything against anyone; so that your Father also who is in heaven may forgive you your transgressions. But if you do not forgive, neither will your Father who is in heaven forgive your transgressions" (Mark 11:25, 26, NASB).

Why is it so hard to forgive? Perhaps part of the reason is that many misunderstand what forgiveness really means.

My oldest son, Terry, while appearing on a TV talk show, gave one of the most concrete definitions of forgiveness I have ever heard. He said, "Forgiveness means that I give up my right to hurt you back.

"But the question always arises," he continued, " 'What if I haven't forgotten?' In his Word God doesn't tell you to forget. He tells you to forgive, and forgiveness is a servant of your will. You *choose* to forgive. So when the negative, hurting memory comes, remind yourself that you have chosen to give up your right to hurt back, and consciously think on other things.

"It's important to remember that anything God has told us to do, we can do. And God has told us to forgive. Once you have decided to do this, you'll find that the memory begins to lose its sting . . . then it will come to mind less and less frequently until it drops out of sight altogether."

If a child is taught to choose forgiveness early in life—and lives with a model who practices it—he is indeed fortunate, for he will grow up free from the blight of bitterness.

The children of a couple I know have suffered lifelong scars because of their parents' mutual unforgiving spirits. Apparently early in their marriage, one of the marriage partners was untrue to his marriage vows. The matter was never settled, never forgiven, never forgotten. The right to hurt back was never relinquished. Consequently, on many occasions as the children were growing up, they often would hear the parents arguing about the indiscretion.

And the absence of forgiveness continues today, even though only one of the couple is still alive. The living parent continues to reinfect the children with memories of bitterness every time the family gathers.

As a result, all of the children have struggled with the problem of unforgivingness, which has hindered the growth of their prayer lives.

Another hindrance to prayer, laziness, is the crying sin of most of us. Prayer is spiritual work, and our human nature does not like to work. It is easier not to pray than to pray.

Yet a desire for God that cannot break the chains of sleep early in the morning will do little good for God. While simply getting up will not in itself bring you closer to God, the overwhelming desire that causes you to break your self-indulgent chains will. And getting up gives vent, increase, and strength to that desire. Indulging yourself by lying in bed will quench the desire. A victory may be lost.

Paul evidently spent much time in prayer for the Ephesian church, that it "might be filled with all the fulness of God" (Eph. 3:18, 19). Epaphras engaged in the exhaustive toil of fervent prayer so that the Colossian church would "stand perfect and complete in all the will of God" (Col. 4:12).

Likewise, each parent, regardless of his circumstances in life, has equal opportunity to travail in prayer until he has birthed his child into "a spirit of wisdom and of revelation in the knowledge of Him" (Eph. 1:17, NASB).

This is spiritually taxing work, and it will cost you

an outlay of serious attention and time. For it takes time for the fullness of God to flow into the spirit. It takes time in the secret places to receive the full revelation of God.

In today's society, few people still choose to pay for quality in merchandise when inferior work will pass just as well in the public eye. This manner of thinking has carried over into our prayer lives. We have so habituated ourselves to meager prayers that they look good to us. At least they quiet our consciences. When we become lax in our prayer lives, we may not realize the peril until the damage has been done.

Jason's parents were regular in their church attendance. They had family devotions in their home—well, at least some of the time. They thanked God for the food—at least on those rare occasions when everybody sat down together. They "always" said bedtime prayers—that is, unless it had been an extra long day.

But one day something they never dreamed could happen to them happened: Jason was arrested for drug abuse. Then Jason's parents dropped to their knees and spent days seeking God in earnest.

How much better to have spent that time in prayer preventing the crisis than correcting it. Christian families are living shabbily because they are praying meagerly! And victories are being won or lost in your life, in your home—in your world—according to *your* prayer life.

The Power of Prayer. Prayer *does* change things, as well as people and circumstances. For example, one public high school I know of had no Christian teachers. A mother whose ninth grader was being taught by an ungodly English teacher began praying that God would change either the man or the situation.

A few months later the English teacher resigned, and a Christian teacher was hired in his place. The same mother also had a four-year-old for whom she began praying that God would provide a Christian kindergarten teacher. Before the child entered school this was accomplished.

Then the mother started a prayer group that met once a week for the stated purpose of praying for their school. God honored those earnest prayers, and within three years three-fourths of the teaching staff of the high school was made up of born-again believers.

During his teen years, my son David was involved in a number of ungodly practices. At the time I was unaware of the specifics, but I knew he was not living for God. And though I had always prayed for our children, I began to seek God fervently on David's behalf. I prayed in the early morning hours. I prayed during the middle of the night. I prayed when I didn't feel like it. I consistently asked God to break the chains of bondage that held my son prisoner.

At first, David seemed to be unaffected by my prayers. And for months, little about him seemed to change. When he brought his ungodly friends home with him they teased him by saying, "Your parents are really 'Christianed-out.' " But they continued to come and often commented on what they called the "different spirit" that permeated our home.

The breakthrough in David's life came suddenly, after several years of no seeming results. One day, with no preamble, David said to Bob, "How can I get close to God? I want to live like you and Mother do."

That was the beginning. From that moment on David's spiritual growth has accelerated. But it didn't happen because I or my husband prayed once or twice. It took a long, concerted effort of prayer.

Prayer for Missions. "God is not hampered by distance," Roger Skinner told us at a missionary conference. "This fact was indelibly impressed on my mind when I was a first-term missionary in Ecuador."

One night Roger answered the phone. The caller was a man who threatened to kidnap the Skinners' one-and-a-half-year-old child. Roger said, "The first thought that flashed into my mind as the caller spoke was, *I wonder who is praying for us today.*"

I was very moved as Roger continued, "It was through *your* prayers that God miraculously kept his hand upon us during those traumatic days." When crises like this occur, he told us, there is no time to contact the home office and request prayer. "For that reason," he said, "if God injects a missionary's name into your thoughts, pause right then and pray for him."

These words deeply impacted me, and consequently, I do make it a practice to pray for those whose names God pops into my mind during the day. Knowing missionaries such as Roger has brought the foreign field of missionary service right into my home, into my personal life. Through men and women like Roger and his wife, I have become vicariously involved in countries and peoples that I will never visit or meet.

Across the years I have invited countless missionaries into our home who, with their families, have left a positive impact on my children. It is, at least in part, a result of these contacts that all of my children have spent considerable time in other areas of the world. At this writing Keith and Heidi are still in Africa sharing God's Word. And David is studying in Israel this year for the purpose of better understanding the Jewish people and culture.

Children who are exposed to the world through the eyes of missionaries will gain a world vision that can't be learned from books alone. I believe every child should have the opportunity to know a missionary family, preferably one with children his age. You might arrange for your children to be prayer partners with some missionary children.

As you consistently hold up these people in prayer, your children will also learn to pray for "their" missionaries. For true to the Genesis Principle, praying parents produce praying children.

GOD'S WORD

The other seed that will bear long-lasting spiritual fruit in your children is the Word of God. "The Word that God speaks is alive and full of power" (Heb. 4:12, AMP). God's Word can act and operate in your home today—if you study it, if you speak it, if you act on it.

To best study God's Word you must set aside certain times to do so. Through my children's growing-up years, I had daily devotions with them every morning. This was an important factor in establishing their personal devotional habits. In my book *The Idea Book for Mothers,* I suggest ways you can incorporate devotional times into your family life.

However, now that all of our children are grown, and those still living at home keep different schedules, we no longer have daily devotions together. But we do set aside one night a week for Bible study. This means everyone comes with his Bible, pencil, and paper. For this weekly time of study, each of us feels free to invite his friends.

How to Study the Bible. I am frequently asked: "How do you study the Bible?"

First, tools are as necessary for a Bible student as they are for a mechanic or carpenter or surgeon. The necessary basics *for even a beginner* include a good Bible (with print large enough to read without strain), a good Bible dictionary, *Strong's Exhaustive Concordance of the Bible* (which will give you the reference of any word in the Bible, as well as its Greek or Hebrew definition), a Bible atlas (which will enable you to trace biblical events), and a sturdy notebook in which to record your growing studies.

Of course, you can begin studying the Bible with

only a few of these tools, but *serious study* will be hampered unless you gather these resources. Other resources will begin to suggest themselves as you go along.

Next, set a regular time and place for your study, where the lighting is good and where your "tools" will be undisturbed by others. Then, just begin.

A good way to start is to study a topic that interests both you and members of your family. Select a subject, then turn to your Strong's concordance and begin following the references that apply to your subject, writing them in your notebook as you look them up.

Compare these Scriptures with each other. Put them into a logical outline as they relate to each other. Meditate on them, asking God to show you what his Word is saying to you. Then begin acting on the new, fresh insights he gives you.

Such studies will change your life and the lives of your children.

In our own home Bible study, because most of our group is college age, we once spent several weeks considering what the Bible had to say about marriage. For example, we read what God said about marriage in the Hebrew culture. We began to see that marriage is defined differently by different cultures, and that what a culture calls marriage is not necessarily the same as what the Bible calls marriage. At the "completion" (no Bible study is ever really completed) of our study on this subject, many of the young people had more questions than answers.

But that study, and others like it, created a thirst within all of us to continue the quest for God's answers.

Don't feel that you must have all the answers for your teenage child. Rather teach him to study in such a manner that for every answer, another question or two will arise.

God is not threatened by any question we might ask him if we are honest in our search. He knows that it's

often the questioner who will become the learner as
he studies and opens himself up to the illumination of
the Holy Spirit.

During another period of time, someone wanted to
know the difference between the Old and New Covenants. These questions resulted in a group study of
God's covenants. We discovered that there are more
than just two covenants that God made between himself and man.

As we were studying the Noahic Covenant (Gen.
6:18; 9:1–17), someone asked whether the rules God
placed on meat eating still apply to us today. Our study
led us to determine that the rules about eating meat
laid down by the Jerusalem Council (Acts 15:19–20,
28–29) are the only mandatory ones for gentile Christians. But, at the same time, the Jewish dietary laws
are certainly relevant and beneficial for those who
choose to live by them.

Do you see what happens in our studies? We are not
trying to discover one absolute interpretation of Scripture to foist upon each other. Instead, we are learning
to apply God's Word in a meaningful way to our lives—
a way in which we can all comprehend something
(some to a small degree and others to a larger degree)
and act upon it. This gives us the freedom to continue
to mature spiritually at our own pace.

My purpose is not to tell you how to interpret God's
Word in your home. Rather I want to encourage you to
share what you know with others, and then encompass
what they share with you. Thus, you will both be
strengthened.

This whole process will teach your children how to
learn to grow in God's Word, rather than to mindlessly
regurgitate a set dogma or creed.

Handling Differences. The meaning a person draws
from the words he reads will depend in part upon his

assumptions, those conclusions that are built upon his personal experiences. For example, consider the variety of answers I received when I asked a group the question, "What is one of the most outstanding characteristics of Jesus?"

The medical student said, "He healed the sick."

"He was a beach preacher," said the surfer. "He often walked along the seashore telling people about God."

"He loved children," said the elementary education major.

"He often got away from others and spent a lot of time by himself," said the loner.

"He spoke boldly to sinners," said the budding evangelist.

"He enjoyed feeding people," said the newly married woman.

"He loved crowds of people," said the city girl.

None of these answers was wrong, yet none encompassed the complete truth about Jesus. We can all agree with Paul: "Now I know in part" (1 Cor. 13:12). No person or parent accurately understands everything God is saying in his Word. For this reason, God has given us his Spirit to lead us into all truth and to teach us all things.

Yet, as a parent, you are also a teacher, and one of your responsibilities is to edify the body of Christ, "till we all come in the unity of the faith" (Eph. 4:13). Can we allow diverse viewpoints in our homes and still keep the "unity of the faith"?

If faith is acting on God's Word, then when your child is acting on the Word that he comprehends and you are acting on the Word that you comprehend, you will have unity. Your comprehension of a particular Scripture may not be exactly the same, but you will both be obedient to the same Lord.

Last year three adult males lived in our home: my

husband, Bob, our son David, and David's cousin John. Bob had committed his life to the Lord a number of years ago; David had done the same about two years previous; John had made Jesus the Lord of his life only within the past few months.

There arose numerous situations in which the three men's application of God's Word to their lives greatly differed.

Bob had the advantage of having walked with the Lord for a number of years. His understanding of the Word was tempered with experience and patience. David's interpretation of some Scriptures was quite strict and legalistic, leaving no room for any but his own application. John was so new to a walk with the Lord that he sometimes accepted the least demanding way to apply the Word to his life.

And yet, because each was sincerely obeying what he understood God's Word was saying to him, he was able to walk in freedom and make great strides in allowing the others to do the same. Thus, we had "unity of the faith" in our home in a practical way.

THE SPOKEN WORD
Peter called the Word of God "incorruptible" seed (1 Pet. 1:23). As believers we are to preach the Word and be witnesses of it. Whenever we speak the Word of God, we actually are sowing its seed in others.

We believe that God intends for us to share the Word together on every occasion, but in our home we have also instituted a special occasion to sow his Word in a concentrated manner: we serve a Friday night Sabbath (Shabbat) meal.

Our community is mostly Jewish and we have become friends with a number of Jewish people. So it was only natural that one couple would invite us to their Sabbath meal one Friday evening. That evening

was so meaningful that we decided to adopt the same
Jewish observance.

After some research, I learned how to set the table
as our Jewish friends did, complete with two Sabbath
candles. I learned how to bake *hallah*, the special
Sabbath bread. I learned the Hebrew prayer to be said
by the mother of the home after the lighting of the
candles, the ceremony that marks the beginning of
the Sabbath.

My husband learned the Hebrew prayers to be said
over the food and over each person present. The latter
prayer, found in Numbers 6:24–26, was given to Moses
by God and commanded to be prayed before the
people. When God finished giving this prayer to Moses,
he said, "And they [Aaron and the priests who were to
pray] shall put my name upon the children of Israel;
and I will bless them" (Num. 6:27).

Our children love the celebration of the Sabbath
meal. We always dress up for the event and usually
invite guests to share it with us. One of the highlights
of the meal is the conversation: it is *Word*-directed.

Early in the week I make the assignment. Everybody
is to share a Scripture verse or passage, and tell what
it means to them. Or maybe I'll suggest that everyone
tell a Bible story and give the reason they like it. Some
of these stories are told in a fresh and dramatic way.
Our guests are told what we are going to share during
the evening so everyone comes prepared.

We also include the additional assignment of sharing
a blessing of the week or day. Then during dessert we
tell what the life of someone who is present has meant
to us.

Our Sabbath meals have become a tradition that we
rarely miss. The table setting is special, the meal is
our finest in the week, and with the conversation
centered around the Word of God, the evening is
always remembered with great joy.

Martha Zimmerman has written a Christ-centered book entitled *Celebrate the Feasts* (Bethany Press, 1981). She gives suggestions to Christians who not only would like to celebrate the Sabbath, but also desire to reenact the Old Testament festivals. This book will provide you with excellent information and guidance.

LIVING GOD'S WORD

Ben, a friend of one of our sons, is a young man who desires to know God's Word. He is very sincere about it. So sincere, in fact, that he walks around quoting Scriptures and saying such things as: "I am the right-eousness of God, so I am righteous. God says I am healed, so I am healed. God tells me I am prosperous, so I'm prosperous. . . . It doesn't *look* like I'm prosper-ous, but I'm not moved by what I see. I'm only moved by what the Bible says."

Yet Ben's car is falling apart and he can't find a job. His clothes are unkempt. He is often sick and was recently hospitalized for a serious condition brought about by his life-style.

As sincere as Ben is, he hasn't yet learned that it's impossible to immediately and permanently overcome every situation simply by quoting Scripture about it. Because the laws of sowing and reaping are always in effect, reading or speaking God's Word will not bring about change *irregardless of your life-style.*

To merely quote Scripture without living in obedi-ence to it is like taking a hybrid seed and laying it on your brick porch. It won't grow. It won't bear fruit. The seed has to be planted according to God's laws of sowing in order for you to reap benefits. And so it is with God's Word. It has to be planted in your life by your actions.

But isn't that what Ben was doing?

Not really. Ben was acknowledging God's Word in a situation. But to activate God's power and promises, he needed to *act upon that Word.*

What does that mean? Part of the answer to this question lies in our confusion between being the righteousness of God and living the righteous life.

When we become Christians by putting our faith in Jesus Christ, we receive the "gift of righteousness" through Jesus Christ (Rom. 5:17) which, at that point in time, is not "by works of righteousness which we have done" (Titus 3:5).

Righteousness, then, is a gift. It is the seed God sows in believers. But then it becomes *our* responsibility to water and nurture that seed so it can grow. As we cultivate the seed, it will produce the harvest of a righteous life. And only in living this righteous life will we experience the reality of the promises Ben so glibly quotes.

During the annual fall revival meetings, the evangelist had frequently moved the people to tears. He closed his final message with this impassioned appeal:

"If you want to be different, if you want your life to be more like Jesus, then come to the altar and commit yourself to him. All it takes is a fresh commitment on your part. Jesus has done so much for you. Won't you now come and give him your life anew?"

In response to the preacher's appeal, Kent, choking with tears, moved to the front to make a new commitment.

However, after a few weeks, Kent realized that he was slipping back into his old ways. He gritted his teeth and vowed, "I *will* keep my commitment. I *will* be stronger. I *will not* live like I used to! I *will* follow Jesus!"

But week by week, his commitment grew weaker and weaker. So during the next revival meetings at church, Kent went forward and made the same commitment to Christ once again. The cycle he set in motion repeated itself many times during the next years.

Kent was sincere enough, and he actually did become the righteousness of Christ at the time he first committed his life to Jesus. But because *he was not taught how to live a righteous life,* he failed again and again.

For example, Kent never understood the sowing and reaping principle. After his commitment to Jesus, nothing much changed about his word input. He did not ingest more of God's Word than of other words. He still spent more time reading the newspaper, watching TV, and idly talking than putting God's Word inside himself. His weak spiritual life reflected its feeding.

In precisely the way that physical health ensues from eating healthy foods, so does spiritual health ensue from eating healthy spiritual food. When you allow the "nutrition" of the Word of God to become a vital, intimate part of your entire system, your relationship with God begins to grow so deep, so full, that other attitudes and words have less and less influence in your life.

In the Hebrew language a righteous man is called a *tzadik.* Such a man is highly regarded by God. "For the Lord knoweth the way of the righteous. . . . And he shall be like a tree planted by the rivers of water, that bringeth forth his fruit in his season; his leaf also shall not wither; and whatsoever he doeth shall prosper" (Ps. 1:6, 3).

By sowing the seeds of obedience to God's Word, you and your children will reap an abundant harvest of righteousness.

4: HOW TO REAP GOOD MANNERS

I was listening intently to our pastor's message, when I heard an abrupt disturbance in the row behind me. "Ouch!" a woman said. "You stepped on my feet." Another voice added, "Hey, careful where you walk."

Without turning, I knew what was happening: it was the Foley children again. Almost every Sunday, at about the same time in the message, one or two of the children would bulldoze their way from the center of the pew to the aisle, heedlessly trampling on everybody's feet in the process. The injured persons were usually strangers because regular attenders avoided sitting near the Foleys.

Minutes later the children all trooped back, and if the owners of the trampled feet were not alert, they would be trampled again during the return. Mrs. Foley would then whisper loudly, "Why do you children *always* do this *every* Sunday?"

After church both parents would berate the children for their behavior, creating an uncomfortable situation for all who happened to be within earshot. From experience I knew that the children acted the same way at other social functions.

Deana Foley was very young and it saddened me to see her growing embarrassment with her children. It seemed the more embarrassed she became, the more she berated her children.

One day when Deana was loudly correcting them, I touched her on the arm.

She looked up and I asked, "May I talk to you a moment?"

"Of course," she said.

I led her to a quiet corner. "Deana," I began, "I don't think your children are deliberately misbehaving...."

"But, Pat," she broke in, "they do it all the time."

"Yes, Deana, I know. But I think they misbehave because they don't know how to behave."

Deana's face reddened. But before she replied I spoke again. "This is a difficult thing for me to tell you, Deana, but I don't think your children are totally to blame."

"What do you mean?"

"Perhaps they just don't know how to act differently."

Tears came to the mother's eyes. "But I try...."
Suddenly she dried her eyes and brightened somewhat. "They aren't really bad children. They just aren't naturally good like yours. But then, your children are older."

That was the opening I had hoped for. "Why don't you bring your children over this week and play some of our 'Polite Games' with us?"

For the next three weeks Deana and her children

came to our home and we role-played proper behavior together. I would describe a situation to the children, then demonstrate how to correctly conduct oneself when it occurred. For example, I would stand in a doorway and instruct the child in the proper way to pass by me.

"When you come to where I am in the doorway," I explained, "instead of just pushing your way past me, you should stop and say, 'Please excuse me,' or, 'May I please go through?'"

Then when the child had passed beside me I taught him to say, "Thank you."

Before long both the children and the mother were beginning to feel comfortable in a number of different situations. Soon an interesting thing began to happen at church. The Foleys began to "fit in" better. Other people stopped avoiding them. And it was simply because they had begun to conduct themselves more mannerly.

Although the change in the Foleys' behavior may seem insignificant to some, it illustrates the importance of planting the right kind of seeds, even the smallest ones. Children, as well as adults, reap appreciation and returned courtesy with each small courtesy that they plant.

MANNERS

Though some would deny it, manners, even the most superficial ones, *are* important. Nobody—unless he is a total recluse—would fail to benefit from exercising a proper, courteous, and likeable approach. Certainly one of the greatest assets any man, woman, or child of God can possess is a warm and winsome conduct.

Everyone might not agree on precise behavior for each particular situation, but most of us would agree upon the fundamental basics of courtesy. And it is the adoption of these basic codes that will produce a harvest of men, women, boys, and girls whose gracious words and actions will draw others to themselves, and ultimately to the Lord whom they represent.

Rather than try to encompass the total range of proper etiquette, this chapter will begin to raise your level of awareness on the subject. It will also illustrate that it's impossible to demonstrate true good manners *outside* your home unless you habitually practice them *within* your home.

In other words, courteous manners become automatic only by continuous, *daily* sowing. You are always planting the seeds of courtesy or discourtesy in your children, and you will inevitably reap in kind from the seeds that you plant. Eventually, good manners will become an integral part of your child's personality and reveal his training—or lack of it.

APOLOGIES

I have heard it said, "Don't ever apologize. Your friends don't need it and others won't receive it." In my opinion, this concept portrays an arrogant attitude that is unworthy of the servant of God.

What is an apology? Are apologies ever necessary?

Basically, an apology is simply telling someone, "I am sorry for what I did or said. I was wrong."

Defined as such, are apologies important?

The answer is a definite yes.

Jesus stressed their importance in Matthew 5:23, 24 (NKJV): "Therefore if you bring your gift to the altar, and there remember that your brother has something against you, leave your gift there before the altar, and go your way. First be reconciled to your brother, and then come and offer your gift."

How much unnecessary hurt and strife would be eliminated if everyone learned to apologize! Most adults find it difficult to ask forgiveness simply because they never learned to make it a part of their automatic system as a child. Some men have been raised to believe that it's just not macho to apologize, that an apology undermines their basic masculinity. Such persons often replant the same seeds of non-apology in their children's lives.

I believe children should receive apologies no matter how young they are. Even a small baby should be apologized to if you have been discourteous to him in some way. Because a child learns his language by what he hears, he learns to apologize by hearing apologies.

For example, suppose your child is playing with a toy in the middle of the floor when you hurriedly enter the room, step on the toy, and break it. What should you do?

Even though the child has chosen a poor place to play with his toy, this is not the time to reprimand him. That would be planting the seeds of non-apology. Instead you might say, "I'm sorry I broke your toy. I should have been more careful to watch where I was walking."

To complete the transaction I would then replace the broken object *as soon as possible.* In so doing, I will have planted an additional seed in my child, the seed of personal responsibility.

If, however, you have broken an irreplaceable object, the situation would need to be handled differently.

You could say, "I know this china doll is irreplaceable. I am very sorry that I was so careless to break it." Then follow up the next day with a written note expressing your regrets, accompanied by something tangible that will please your child. You will have taught him that even though some losses are irreplaceable, it is important to make up for the damage in another way.

My young neighbor who visited me is a good exam-

ple of someone who instills these principles. I served
Gloria and Tommy grape juice. As Tommy drank his
juice, he spilled some on my tablecloth. He told me,
"I'm sorry." Instead of making a fuss about the accident, I removed the tablecloth and put it to soak.

The following day both the mother and Tommy
came over to see if I had been able to remove the stain
from the tablecloth. When they entered my home the
child handed me a bouquet of flowers. "I'm sorry I
spilled juice on your tablecloth," he said. "And I picked
some flowers for you."

I was pleased with the way the mother had handled
the whole situation. Not only had she trained Tommy
to act appropriately at the moment he spilled the
juice, but she had taught him to realize that his responsibility did not necessarily end with an apology—
as important as that was.

COMPLIMENTS

What is a compliment? I noticed this definition in
Webster's dictionary: "formal and respectful recognition." Everyone needs recognition from someone.
Nobody is exempt from this universal need. And the
recognition that counts the most comes from the ones
we love the most.

Try an experiment. If you haven't recently complimented someone close to you—your wife, husband,
parent, or child—do so today. Spend a few minutes
determining what you will say. Make your words a
genuine affirmation of the person's worth to you. In
other words, as in the above definition, show respectful
recognition for who or what they are.

When you speak these words of appreciation, say
them in a manner that reflects the person's value to
you. Don't in any way lessen the impact of your words
by flippancy or lightness. Convey to that person in the

very best way you can that you respect, love, and appreciate them.

Notice the warm, happy response that comes to
their eyes. You will find yourself warmed, too, and your
relationship with the person strengthened. Now that
you've complimented them once, why not make it a
regular practice?

Giving and receiving positive feedback is so fraught
with difficulties that many adults are unable to honestly engage in the process. By keeping silent, we
reinforce each other's self-doubts.

Most of us know our weaknesses. They cling to us
like parasites. And all too frequently we focus attention
on those weaknesses, which only enlarges and
nourishes them.

For example, how often have you heard a woman
say, "I'm a terrible cook. . . . I'm a very poor house-
keeper. . . ." Or a man say, "I'll never get a raise this
year. . . . I'm getting so soft that I can't lift the things I
used to. . . ."

No wonder we hear our children saying such things
as, "Aw, I can never learn to spell. . . . Algebra is too
hard for me. . . ."

Parents have the power—and the responsibility—to
teach their offspring to think highly of themselves.
One way to accomplish this is by telling children that
they can succeed in anything they set themselves to
do, then providing incremental compliments to encourage them along the way.

A college classmate of mine took a typing job one
summer after having only one semester of typing. At
the end of her first day of work, the professor for
whom she was typing came out of his office and
approached her desk.

"I just want to tell you how pleased I am with your
work," he said.

The professor's words startled Jackie. She believed

she was such a poor typist that she had worked through her lunchtime that day in order to turn in a "reasonable" amount of work.

Jackie says she can still remember the long silence that followed the professor's words. She was so unused to receiving compliments and so unsure of herself, that she immediately thought, *He's being sarcastic and doesn't like my work.*

So she didn't know whether she should say, "Thank you"—in case the professor had been sincere—or, "I'll try harder tomorrow"—in case he was getting ready to fire her.

Since most of us generally judge ourselves more harshly than others do, we, like Jackie, tend to "hear" criticism where none exists. This readily accounts for the fact that very early in life many children become ill at ease—even anxious or suspicious—when they receive a compliment.

The reason is obvious. As with everything else, it's impossible to harvest a crop that has not been planted.

When I was in high school, our pastor had a young daughter with lovely long, brown, braided hair. Once I complimented her on her hair in her father's presence. His immediate reaction was, "Rachael, you look so untidy, it's embarrassing."

Then, speaking directly to me, he said, "Don't ever comment on Rachael's looks. I will not allow her to grow up thinking she's attractive. That's a tool of the devil."

All people flourish in an atmosphere of approval, but wither and die in an atmosphere of disapproval. None is more vulnerable in this area than our children. Therefore, we must be very alert to compliment them on their strengths and not focus on their weaknesses.

The end result of our neglect to do this is to plant the seeds of self-doubt in our children. This doubt spawns a host of other problems, including inability to give and receive compliments.

Conversely, our children will learn to give compliments by hearing us express appreciation not only to them, but also to others.

A salesgirl shows you unusual courtesy, or is particularly patient in serving you. Do you mention it appreciatively? Spend a moment and tell her so. The girl's feet probably hurt, and her spirit may be low.

You enjoy your dinner in a restaurant. Do you tell the waiter? He must get terribly tired of serving food all day to people who only find fault.

One of your children gets a good mark on a school paper. Do you show your pride and appreciation by sitting down with the child and going over the paper, expressing your pleasure over each right answer?

On a rainy day, your spouse makes a tasty pot of chili. Do you comment on how it warms you?

Your paper boy places the newspaper on the porch out of the rain. Do you express your appreciation to him?

Money alone cannot pay for especially cheerful or efficient service, or for a particularly fine job. And it takes only a few seconds to say a heartwarming "thank you." We all remember the story in Luke 17 of Jesus healing the ten lepers. Yet only one of those healed men returned to give thanks. Jesus noticed the omission and asked, "Were there not ten cleansed? But where are the nine?" (Luke 17:17).

Aim to be like the leper who returned. Planting seeds of appreciation is largely a matter of cultivating the habit of noticing the many, many ways people around you make a contribution to your life—and then expressing it.

CONVERSATION
Conversation, or oral communication, is the result of comprehending and sharing the same meanings of certain words or concepts. To communicate effectively

requires both mental and physical effort.

Conversation rarely breaks down for our lack of desire to communicate. Most of us want to be understood, often desperately so, but sometimes find it difficult to verbally express ourselves. Children need to be taught the fundamentals of conversation enough to comfortably engage in it. An aid that I find useful in teaching the basics of conversation is a game I call "Catch Talk."

To begin, seat the child on the floor, toss him a ball, and ask him to toss it back. Throw it back and forth a few times. Then toss the ball and tell the child to keep it in his lap. Toss him another ball to hold in his lap, then a third and a fourth. Now put your hands in your lap and sit there. When you do this, the child may become uncomfortable. He will probably say, "We're not playing anymore."

"That's right," you respond, "we're not. In order to play catch ball, you have to catch the ball, then toss it back to me. You play Catch Talk the same way. When someone throws you a sentence or question, you have to catch it and throw one back. Let's try it. OK?"

"OK."

"If I asked you if you had fun at Sandy's yesterday, what would you say?" I asked.

"Yes."

"Did you play with his trains?"

"Yes."

"Did you remember to thank Mrs. Rath for inviting you?"

"Yes."

Now stop and repeat the questions and answers, tossing a ball with each question and instructing your child to keep it in his lap. Explain how he had caught the "talk" balls you threw him by answering "yes." But he had not thrown the "talk" ball back. Suggest that you try the first question again.

"Did you have fun at Sandy's yesterday?"

"Yes."

"OK, you've caught the ball. Now what could you say to throw a "talk" ball back to me? How about telling me one thing you played?"

"We played with his dog."

"What fun that must have been. Mrs. Rath told me that Sandy's dog does tricks."

"Yes, he plays sleeping. He sits up, and he brings sticks back to you when you throw them."

"That makes a fun game, just like the fun we're having by throwing sentences back and forth to each other."

Within a few minutes, your child will begin to see the connection between the two games. The seeds of conversing, like other seeds, require regular nurturing until they fully mature.

A communication game that is helpful with an older child is one I call "Your Body's Conversation." One person describes a behavior he observes in another player, then guesses the reason for the behavior.

For example, the first player might say, "I see you smile, and I imagine that you are enjoying this game." Or, "I see you fold your arms and move back, and I imagine that you are bored with this game."

The other player will then validate or repudiate your conclusion as follows: "No, actually I was thinking about a joke I heard last night." Or, "Yes, I am bored. I don't see the purpose of this exercise."

"Your Body's Conversation" illustrates how easy it is for us to misjudge another's motives without sufficient communication. Taking time to play a game like this with your child teaches him that more is involved in a conversation than just saying words.

Another way to encourage your child's conversational gifts is to ask him insightful questions. Because many people have never learned to ask intelligent questions they are at loss to discourse on subjects they know little or nothing about. By your example and encouragement, your children will learn to explore new topics.

This is very important, for a child who can ask meaningful questions will grow up to be a comfortable conversationalist. What better way is there to show your interest in others than to ask them appropriate questions? What better way is there to show a person that God is interested in him than for you to be interested in him?

CORRESPONDENCE

Many people will evaluate us on the basis of the letters we write. And though we can't choose their evaluations, we can certainly determine their "ammunition."

Are your letters friendly, chatty, newsy? Do they discuss only people? Or do they also discuss ideas? Do they focus on yourself and your personal interests? Or also on the recipient and his needs? Are they gloomy and negative? Or cheerful and positive?

Charles Colson tells of a ninety-year-old woman, living in a rest home, who brings joy and hope to scores of prisoners by her uplifting letters. When Mr. Colson visited this woman who is so important to so many, he found her sitting alone in a scantily furnished room, happily responding to her "boys."

Though this woman had every right to give up and succumb to despair, she chose to inspire others by sharing the love of Jesus with them.

What kind of a letter writer are you?

Every letter deserves an answer, unless it is a response to yours. And the sooner you reply, the easier it is. It is better to write a few lines by return mail than to send a four-page letter a month later. But it is better to write a year later than not at all.

The above paragraph is directed at myself. It is a message I frequently have to preach to myself. I receive letters from many people, most of whom I don't know. But I firmly believe that if someone has been courteous enough to write to me, I must be courteous enough to respond.

My children began writing letters—giving special attention to "Thank Yous"—as soon as they were able to hold a pencil or crayon in their hand and draw. There are no excuses for failure to send *immediate* thank-you notes for gifts, favors, and invitations. Neglect in this area is a serious breach of good manners, since it shows disrespect for the feelings of others.

Because my children developed the habit of writing letters early in their lives, they are excellent correspondents now as adults. Each has his own personal style and flavor, but all write as an automatic procedure.

My daughter Alíce is especially fond of sending carefully selected greeting cards, both for special days as well as for those ordinary days that need to be made special. Alíce rarely uses a card for an excuse not to write, for she usually encloses a newsy note.

Few things brighten a day for anyone like cheery mail. For many people, especially the lonely and shut-ins, correspondence is another reminder of God's love and his remembrance of them.

For those of you who already have a card ministry or desire to start one, many Christian card companies offer an excellent selection of creative, God-honoring, all-occasion cards. One that I recommend is the Mustard Seed Co. (Three Rivers, MI).

Another hint: Although it's acceptable to type personal letters, letters of condolence, congratulations, or thanks should always be handwritten.

My daughter-in-law Heidi elects to keep in touch with picture postcards. During the past year, as she and Keith have been traveling and ministering throughout the Middle East and Africa, Heidi has written hundreds of picture postcards from different countries. What a magnificent way of keeping family, friends, and prayer partners continually updated concerning their activities for the Lord.

However, even more important than the information those cards transmit is the underlying message: "I'm thinking of you. You're important to me."

It's much easier to share the power of God in your life when people feel like you really care about them and know you make an effort to keep in touch.

Those of you who are often on the go can redeem the time during those unscheduled delays by keeping several stamped postcards on hand. Carry a few of these cards in your purse, briefcase, or glove compartment. Then when God puts a thought in your mind to be shared with a friend, you can do so quickly and conveniently.

In chapter 3 I suggested choosing missionary children to be prayer partners for your children. Now I would like to suggest that you and your children make your prayer partners your pen pals as well. Did you notice that I said *you* and your children? Even in this kind of correspondence, your children will do better if they have a good model. So parents, find yourself a missionary pen pal. If you don't know any, ask your pastor or write to your denominational headquarters for recommendations.

"Good news from far away is like cold water to the thirsty," reads Proverbs 25:25 (TLB), a good reminder that's so very applicable to our missionaries. Each of us is responsible to give that cold water in the name of Jesus. Remember, those who go to share the Good News in a foreign land are often going in our stead. You and I and our children can lift our missionaries' spirits and remind them we care. And how shall we do this? With *today's* letter!

Children who cannot write letters, either because

they have not developed creative letter writing skills or because they do not write legibly, are communicatively handicapped.

What a thrill it is for anyone to receive a letter that has been thoughtfully, creatively written. And how wonderful to learn to write such a letter, one designed to increase the reader's comfort (illegible handwriting does not contribute to comfort!), to hold his interest, and to add to his store of knowledge or understanding. When one realizes that the primary purpose of letter writing is to meet the needs of the reader, he will bend his efforts toward that worthwhile goal.

DINING

Many Christian homes display plaques in their dining areas that read, "Christ is the Head of our house, the unseen Guest at every meal." In some such homes, as I have seen the careless way food and dishes are put on the table, I've wondered how the dwellers in that home would feel if their unseen Guest were suddenly to manifest himself physically.

As I prepare my meals and make my table attractive, I find it helps me to always keep in mind these words, "Whatever you do in word or deed, do all in the name of the Lord Jesus, giving thanks to God and the Father through Him" (Col. 3:17, NKJV).

Our tables and our meals always ought to be prepared in such a manner that we would not be ashamed to entertain our Lord. Because only when we arrange our table and prepare our food for his honor do we properly do it for our family.

As soon as my own children were old enough to set the table, I borrowed some library books with pictured table settings and taught them a variety of proper ways to do it. Young children love the confidence that comes from knowing how to do something just right, and correctly setting a table is no exception.

Have you ever noticed that your family's table manners are affected by the way the table and food are presented? Experience has taught me that children who develop correct table manners usually come from a home that has a "correct table" from which to learn them.

As I mentioned in chapter 3, our regular Sabbath dinners are done in our best style. Everyone dresses up in his good clothes. The table is spread with a lovely tablecloth and fancily folded napkins. We use our best dishes, crystal, individual bread and butter dishes, and formally arranged silverware. Each male seats the lady or ladies on his right. One of the children is chosen to assist me in serving from the left and taking away from the right.

During a formal dinner like this, as well as at other meals, children should be taught not to talk with food in their mouths. Quite importantly, children need to learn to watch the hostess, to wait for her to begin eating, and to follow her example in eating.

If blunders or accidents occur, they never should be brought to the attention of others. These incidents should be addressed in private after the meal.

Dinners in which correct manners are practiced are not only pleasurable for all concerned, but also excellent training grounds. Children can go from meals like these with the confidence that they will feel at ease in any company.

It is crucial that good table manners become automatic. Never allow your children to develop bad habits at your family dinner table. If you do, they will become confused when you insist on good manners when a guest arrives. If they are taught consistency in their table manners, they will be comfortable with their eating habits under any circumstances.

Remember that the main purpose of table conversation is to provide positive stimulation. Emotionally disturbing talk should never be allowed at the table. Make your meal a time of meaningful communication so that your child will anticipate food for his total being when he comes to the table.

Our children were taught never to leave the table without saying, "May I please be excused?" Upon receiving an affirmative answer, they would then thank me for the meal. They were not required to add descriptive adjectives such as "good lunch" or "yummy food" unless they chose to do so. But the habitual courtesy of expressing appreciation to the one who had prepared their food planted a seed that matured into a spirit of gratefulness.

You might want to set aside a meal every once in a while to specifically discuss table etiquette. Most children—and young people, too, as I have learned—are eager to know how to properly conduct themselves at tables.

I can never forget the young man who was our guest for several months this past year. One evening after our Sabbath dinner, he came to me with tears in his eyes. "Pat, I just want to thank you for teaching me proper table manners," he said. "All of my life I've been self-conscious when eating around people I admire."

He took a deep breath before going on. "But now, at last, I'm at ease. I can concentrate on the people I'm eating with rather than my own shortcomings."

It takes an effort to set your table nicely. It takes an effort to plan and prepare a centerpiece. It takes an effort to wash and iron linen napkins. It takes an effort to take the bread out of the wrapper and place it in a bread basket. It takes an effort to pour milk into a pitcher.

It takes an effort to plant and nurture seeds in a garden until they produce food *fit for a king*. And it takes an effort to plant and nurture seeds in a young life until he develops into a mature child of God who

will someday share a table *with a King.*
But it's worth it.

LISTENING

Listening is not merely a passive activity. Proper listening is as much a developed skill as good manners. In
listening that deserves the name, all of one's senses
are brought to bear upon the speaker. One listens with
his eyes as well as with his hands. A truly good listener
hears with his whole body.

When David was small and learning to talk, I sometimes did as all mothers do. I tried to bake or do some
other household chore while attempting to listen to
him.

David would have none of that. More than once he
would tug on my dress or apron. "Mother, look at me.
Look at my eyes so you can hear what I'm saying!"

I'm reminded of the little boy who had come back
from a birthday party. He excitedly tried to tell his
mother what had happened. Being in the midst of
dinner preparations, she absentmindedly said, "I'm
busy, Jeff. Go tell your father."

But his father was reading the newspaper. So he
tried to talk to one of his brothers, who was so busy
with his homework that he sent Jeff away, too. Discon-
solate, Jeff sat down on the back steps with his dog. As
his mother went to the door to call him for dinner she
heard him say somewhat sadly, ". . . and we had chocolate ice cream, too. . . ."

At our house, if someone isn't being appropriately
attentive, a family member only needs to softly say,
"And we had chocolate ice cream, too." It brings about
an immediate refocus of priorities.

When your child, or anyone else, is talking to you,
you should afford him your complete attention. Look
directly into his eyes, nod your head now and then,
and make brief comments without actually interrupt-

ing. Smile or laugh when it is appropriate. Assume a grave expression if the news is serious. And take out a pencil and paper if you are being asked to do a favor or run an errand to indicate that you want to remember.

Whatever you do, determine *not* to follow the example of one executive I knew. When people came into his office to discuss a business or personal matter, Charlie would pull out one of his desk drawers and begin organizing it.

Needless to say, Charlie soon had few interruptions, few encroachments upon his time. I wasn't surprised to learn that his tenure with the company was not long. Apparently his rude manner of listening exhibited itself too often or to the wrong person.

Parents should alert each other when they observe the symptoms of inattentive listening. Some of the most apparent symptoms are these: letting your eyes wander around the room or beyond your child, interrupting your child before he finishes a sentence, and changing the subject without acknowledging his ideas.

Remember that a child's self-concept is an extremely fragile thing. It is threatened when his parents do not listen to him, and greatly enhanced when they do.

A much-debated topic among psychologists is whether parents have a greater effect upon their children by the way they listen or by the way they instruct.

Actually, it matters little which has the greater effect, because in both areas we are planting seeds, and planting them daily. So if you find yourself saying to your child, "Why don't you ever listen?" pause and ask yourself who planted the seeds of inattentiveness.

RESPECT

Respect is the essence of all good manners, for it simply means consideration. In one of many references to the subject, God's Word speaks of respect this way,

". . . in honour preferring one another" (Rom. 12:10).

Honoring our father and mother is "the first commandment with promise" (Eph. 6:2). The Jewish rabbis say this responsibility includes rising when they enter the room, not correcting or publicly disagreeing with them, and being considerate of their needs.

Every culture and every age dictates in large part how people behave socially. The United States is no exception. And in this country, during the past two or three decades, the emphasis has swung from community or family to self—individual freedom. "I gotta be me!" is the cry. "I want to do *my thing.*" We see the results of that sowing all around us.

In contrast, the Bible and the Jewish culture emphasize community. "Love your neighbor as yourself," God told us in Leviticus 19:18 (TLB), a commandment Jesus repeated in the Gospels. Loving one's neighbor is respect in action. It opens the doors of one's heart to another. In a very practical sense, respect also opens other doors. . . .

A man can show respect for a woman in public by opening a door for her and letting her pass in front of him. The exceptions to this procedure occur in a train or bus where the gentleman is to open the door and disembark first, then hold out his hand to help the lady. A young woman can show respect by doing the same for an elderly gentleman or woman.

As our children were growing up, the boys were taught to open the doors for their sisters and to walk along the street side of the sidewalk when accompanying them. All this was *planting seeds, planting seeds, planting seeds.*

Children should learn never to enter a closed room without first knocking on the door and awaiting an invitation. Parents should model this behavior for their children. From early childhood on, as soon as he desires it, every child's right to personal privacy should be respected.

We sometimes fail to realize how important a child's personal belongings are to him. But when we treat our child's valuables with respect, we provide him further lessons in how to respect the rights, privileges, and property of others.

This same respect should be accorded the men and women who make and enforce our laws. Children learn their basic respect (or non-respect) of authority from their models, their parents. "Let every soul be subject unto the higher powers," God says. "For there is no power but of God" (Rom. 13:1). And again, "Obey them that have the rule over you" (Heb. 13:17).

These statements from God's Word apply to both civil and ecclesiastical authorities.

A friend of mine was driving a carful of young people to a summer youth camp. Some of the children in the car were from an economically depressed area of the city, and they spoke angrily and disrespectfully about "the law." Henry rebuked them kindly, but firmly. "Those men are our friends and protectors," he said. He failed to convince the most vocal of the children, however.

As they were driving through a large northern California city, Henry took an incorrect turn and found himself driving the wrong way on a one-way street. The time was early evening and the streets were full of commuter traffic. Everyone in the car instantly recognized the danger.

Before Henry could rectify the situation, a traffic officer pulled alongside him. Henry rolled down his window and said, "I'm sorry, sir. I was unfamiliar with the street. . . ."

The officer smiled. "That's alright. Happens to all of us." Then he held up his hand, stopped traffic, and helped Henry turn around and head in the right direction.

There was complete silence from the dissenter for the rest of the trip. He had learned a valuable lesson.

Another opportunity to show respect comes to all of us almost daily. Anytime you find yourself in a group of people that is talking disparagingly about someone you know, you can easily say something kind, or at least tolerant. It is surprising how often just one favorable comment will cause another to speak up and add something to what you have said. And so the conversation takes a turn and ends by giving a good name to the person under discussion. And one of the most precious things a person can possess is a good name.

Our son David was a guest at an Orthodox Jewish Passover. He had the privilege of being seated with a young rabbi whose wife and five children were also present. During the course of the meal, David spoke to the rabbi's wife. "Your children are so well-behaved . . . and so knowledgeable. You must begin to train them when they are very young."

The young mother acknowledged his compliment with a smile, then said, "No, before they are born."

In exactly the same way a gardener chooses the seeds he plants in order to reap the harvest he wants, so do wise parents who seek to reap good manners sow them in their children.

5: HOW TO REAP PRODUCTIVE STEWARDSHIP

Three men sat in the businessman's outer office. "I wonder why the boss wants to see us," one said.

"I wish I knew," the second man said in a nervous tone.

The third man was relaxed. "I think the boss is going to give us a special job to do."

Just at that moment the door opened and the boss said, "Come in, fellows. Have a seat."

After they were all comfortably seated, Cyrus said, "Men, I'm going to take a trip of indefinite length, and I want to entrust some of my belongings to your care while I'm gone."

Before the men could answer, Cyrus handed each one a heavy pouch. "Take care of this the best way you know how," he said. "I'm leaving immediately; you'll be notified when I return." He arose and the meeting was over.

When the men opened their bags, they were astonished to find them full of money. Jacob quickly counted the gold coins in his bag. He whistled. "Wow! Fifty thousand dollars!"

Andrew poured a stack of gold upon the table. "I've got twenty thousand!" he said in astonishment.

The third man, named Issachar, had been with Cyrus just a short time. He had been given the responsibility of caring for ten thousand dollars.

Their faces wreathed with joy, Jacob and Andrew quickly departed, making plans to invest their boss's money. "Are you coming, Issachar?" Jacob asked.

Issachar shook his head. "No, I've got to think."

After the others had gone, Issachar sat very still for a long time staring at the dull glitter of ten thousand dollars' worth of gold, the most he had ever seen at one time. After a while he heaved a heavy sigh and rose to his feet.

Making certain he was not followed, Issachar slunk down the back streets on his way home. There he picked up a shovel and started out the back door.

"What are you going to do?" his wife asked.

"I'm afraid to keep this money in the house," he said. "And I know my boss would be furious if I lost it. So I'm going to bury it. It'll be safer that way."

Some months later, when he returned, the boss *was* furious, but for a different reason than Isaachar thought. Cyrus called the three men into his office again. Looking tanned and rested, he said, "Well, men, how did you fare with the money I entrusted into your care?"

Jacob excitedly hefted two huge bags to the table. "I invested the fifty thousand dollars," he said, "and *doubled* your money."

"Well done, Jacob!" Cyrus said. "I'm promoting you

to the head of your department. With a substantial raise," he added.

Cyrus looked at Andrew. Andrew strained to lift one very heavy bag to the table. "Sir, I invested the twenty thousand dollars, and I also *doubled* the money you gave to me. Here it is."

"Well done, Andrew!" Cyrus said. "Congratulations! You, too, have earned a promotion and a raise in salary."

All three men turned to look at Issachar who was trembling as he carefully brushed the fresh soil from his bag and laid it on the table. When he told his boss what he had done, Cyrus was angry. "You knew I would at least expect this money to earn interest, Issachar. You have betrayed my trust in you."

In this dramatization of the parable Jesus told in Matthew 25:14-30, we can quickly see that he was teaching us that good stewards are faithful and productive. It isn't the *size* of one's resources that matters to the Lord as much as the *manner* in which they are used. No matter what our level of finances or personal giftedness may be, we are all given the *same responsibility,* the same opportunity for reward, as those three stewards. As a parent, you have an unparalleled opportunity for teaching this truth to your children.

STEWARDSHIP OF OUR MONEY

What does God tell us to do with the money he has entrusted to us? Turning to his Word, we find some general guidelines.

"Will a man rob God?" God asks. Then, answering his own question, he says, "Yet ye have robbed me. . . . In tithes and offerings. . . . Bring ye all the tithes into the storehouse . . ." (Mal. 3:8, 10).

What is God talking about? What is a tithe?

At the outset, God's tithe came into being for two purposes: (1) to care for the Levites and priests so they could give their full attention to spiritual leadership, and (2) to care for the poor. The New Testament does not give any indication that these priorities ever changed.

Unfortunately, our second obligation sometimes receives little attention. Yet God says: "For the poor shall never cease out of the land: therefore I command thee, saying, Thou shalt open thine hand wide unto thy brother, to thy poor, and to thy needy . . ." (Deut. 15:11).

God's Word specifies the need for his people to care for the poor. The writings of the rabbis say that of all the ways to assist the poor, the highest degree of charity is to provide work for them so they can become self-supporting.

My husband and I became aware of God's imperative to help the poor in relation to a Spanish-speaking family in our city. Anna, her husband, and their three children came to Los Angeles from Guatemala. Anna speaks practically no English, and Fernando fares little better. They live with another family in a tiny apartment. Fernando has had difficulty finding work, and when we first met Anna, the family was in sore straits. In the Los Angeles area, there are hundreds and hundreds of such families, but the Lord spoke to us about this particular one.

Neither Anna nor her husband wanted a handout, they merely wanted a "hand-*up.*" We called a family conference to discuss how we could help. At the time we had several college-age young people living at "Camp Palisades," as our home is frequently called. Because we had already divided up our work load, we really didn't need outside assistance with the housework. But the consensus was, "Let's each contribute several dollars a week and hire Anna to do some housework."

So it was agreed. Though none of us could easily afford it, we decided to minister to this family by providing Anna a job that would enable her to earn a day's income and also give her a future work reference.

At first, we intended to have Anna clean only a couple of times a month. But when we realized how desperately the family needed money, we decided to have her come each week. In response to our under-standing of the biblical imperative, we pay her adequately—in fact, about twice the legal minimum wage. At present, Anna is enrolled in an English class and she and her family have a growing sense of be-longing both to this country and to the worldwide family of God.

In response to God's specific command to care for the fatherless and widows (Deut. 14:29; James 1:27), Bob and I also have accepted responsibility for a score of homeless children in Korea, the Philippines, and Hong Kong through an organization we have founded. LUV-A-CHILD helps provide housing, food, clothing, and education for these children in a Christian environ-ment in the child's own homeland. (For complete information, write LUV-A-CHILD, P.O. Box 411, Pacific Palisades, CA 90272.)

We also follow the example given in Jesus' parable in Luke 14:21, 22. Twice each year, at Easter and Thanksgiving, we fill our home with as many as thirty guests. Though we do invite a few friends, we make a point to invite several who are lonely or poor and cannot return the favor by inviting us to their homes.

Since our family is careful about the food that enters these temples of the living God, we enjoy this opportu-nity to prepare and share recipes of many tasty, nutri-tious foods.

Seed Faith Giving. You may be familiar with "seed faith giving," a concept of financial giving designed after one of God's laws of sowing and reaping: "Give, and it shall be given unto you; good measure, pressed down, and shaken together, and running over, shall men give into your bosom. For with the same measure that ye mete withal it shall be measured to you again" (Luke 6:38).

Initially, the inevitable effect of generosity is a return on one's investment. But if one's motive for giving is only to receive, it is like planting seed in ground that is never fed. The ground will produce a harvest for a while, but the harvest will begin to grow skimpier and skimpier from lack of nutrients. This is exactly what will happen to your seed faith giving if it is not nurtured by prayer and obedience to God's Word.

Once you have planted the seed, keep nurturing it by prayer, just as a farmer watches over his crop. But don't stop there. Don't watch the newly planted seed to the exclusion of planting and nurturing other crops in other fields.

Giving is a command, not an emotionally generated action. So pray and ask God to show you where and to whom you should give. The biblical directive is *"Every man according as he purposeth in his heart,* so let him give; not grudgingly, or of necessity: for God loveth a cheerful giver" (2 Cor. 9:7, emphasis added).

Then, after you have given prayerfully and obediently, handle the balance of your monies as something also entrusted to you by God. He will hold us fully accountable for our use of all his gifts.

A Pitfall to Avoid. Don't give beyond your means! We did, and floundered because of it. We somehow have found ourselves on the mailing lists of many ministries and, more than once, have been drawn into giving beyond our ability.

A case in point: One very urgent mail appeal touched us emotionally. So we gave several hundred dollars to the ministry, forcing some of our creditors to wait for their justly owed monies. In this particular case, the money was not ours to give.

When we later analyzed our action, we realized that we had given for one or all three of the following reasons: (1) We had been moved by the appeal. (2) We had sincerely desired to help. (3) We had hoped to receive a hundredfold return—in the same legal tender—on our investment in the Kingdom of God.

Much wiser now that we have evaluated both motives and actions, we are learning to give sanely, but even more importantly, *prayerfully.*

As we understand the parable of the talents, it seems clear that Jesus is telling his people that if they *properly handle and distribute* what they have, God will provide even more to care for. But if we carelessly handle our goods, he will allow even those goods to be taken away.

Therefore, we are doing the best we know with what we have. There is still so very much that we don't know about handling money. For that reason—just as we are doing in other areas of our lives in which we lack knowledge—we are praying that God will send someone to help teach us.

If you have been a poor steward of your finances up to this point, it's not too late to start again. Determine to change for the better *today,* being grateful that God in his mercy has not taken away what you have. However, don't be deceived into continuing your irresponsible ways. For God is not mocked, and you *will reap* according to what you sow. And one of the ways you will reap is in the financial habits of your children.

Teaching Your Children about Money. Recently my daughter Alíce and I were in a television rental establishment. We saw a woman, accompanied by her cute two-year-old son, choosing home video movies.

The clerk had just totaled the amount of their selections when the tiny boy spoke up. "Charge it," he said. "Just put it on our card."

In our society, children are exposed to credit at a very early age. They see their parents "paying with plastic" long before they even understand what money is. All too often this ignorance continues as they grow older, and they learn no connection between incurring bills and paying them.

Children need to be taught how to handle money. They need to understand how interest on unpaid bills works. They need to understand how costly this extra charge can become when the original debt begins to compound itself at the rate of 18 percent or more. And it is the parents' responsibility to teach them.

One father I know opens a checking account for his children when they reach age twelve. He deposits money to cover the cost of school lunches, recreation, and visits to the dentist. Then he teaches the children how to write their own checks and balance their checkbooks.

Another set of parents allows their junior high school child to share the bill-paying chore by writing checks for the parents' signature. This plan has proven to be a better eye-opener about the costs of goods and services than any lecture they could give him.

The Educational Employees Credit Union in Fort Worth, Texas, has created a savings group called the Buckaroos for seven- to thirteen-year-olds. New members up to age eleven get a tour of the credit union and some basic money-management lessons. Twelve- and thirteen-year-olds who deposit at least twenty-five dollars (there's no minimum balance thereafter) get a free checking account, together with an hour-long training course on how to write checks and balance a

checkbook. You might see if a financial institution in
your area offers such a program.

A credit union in Topeka, Kansas, gives loans on
bicycles to children under the age of seventeen. With a
maximum loan of two hundred dollars (cosigned by
parents) to be repaid in one year, Kansas Credit Union
hopes to teach young people the basics of money
management while building customers for the future.

Some parents let their children play with old can-
celed checks. Preschoolers can learn to read numbers
from these slips of paper and will grasp the idea that
this is a way of paying for things. Your child will also
receive an inside look at your value system by learning
what you write checks for.

Another father cashes his paycheck, then sits down
with his whole family to pay the bills. They make
stacks of currency and bills. The children are allowed
to place the necessary money in an envelope with the
bill. In addition to learning how to handle finances,
these children never beg their parents for extra money.
They have learned firsthand how much money has
been entrusted into their care and exactly how the rest
of it is spent.

STEWARDSHIP OF OUR TIME
"What time is it?"
   "If only I had time. . . ."
   "I don't know where the time has gone."
   Sound familiar? Of course, we've all said them. But
even as we speak those words, we can hear, if we
listen, the continuing refrain from God's Word, "redeeming the time," "redeeming the time," "redeeming
the time" (Eph. 5:16).

A good steward redeems the time, he does not own
it. Time is not parceled out in bundles with our names
on it. We cannot claim of time, "This is mine" in the

same way that we can with our possessions. It is only redeemed time that can be retained.

One of the definitions Webster's dictionary gives for *redeem* is "to save in any manner." Think about that for a moment. It's good. Time is only ours when we save it.

There are many different ways for you to save your time. And it's not too important which ways you choose. It only matters that you do it, because time is the stuff that life is made of.

Setting Goals. One of the most frequent complaints I hear from mothers is "I don't feel as though I accomplished anything today (or this week). I was busy all the time but I don't know what I did. It makes me feel that I'm not doing anything constructive."

All of us feel this way when we are not redeeming the time, regardless of our profession.

I have learned that I need to set goals in order to most effectively use my time. By writing out my goals, I can review them regularly to check my progress. Personally, I find that my daily direction tends to become muddled unless I know my long-term goals.

Making and reviewing goals may seem cumbersome to you at first, but it is just like any other unfamiliar process—difficult at first, easier as it goes along. Do you remember when you first learned to drive a car? It seemed you had too many things to do and remember at once. You consciously thought about every move, every action. It was difficult, wasn't it? Difficult and well nigh impossible. But when you had driven several times, each process gradually became automatic, literally a part of your automatic behavior. It will be the same with goal setting.

Once you have set your goals, you can develop a written system of daily planning. For example, I organize my day by making a list of everything that has to be done. Then I prioritize the list and start marking off the items as I do them, usually handling the most unpleasant task first and the most pleasant last.

The value of this habit for me is that, even amidst multitudinous interruptions, I get more accomplished. My day actually becomes more enjoyable as it goes along. This system also helps me to eliminate procrastination, which is the downfall of many who desire to be good stewards of time.

Bob, on the other hand, usually makes long lists and works on the items in the order of their importance. Most days he does not get completely through the list, but he doesn't feel pressured because he knows that he is always working on what is most important. Every so often, he will take a few hours and clean up leftover lists.

Remember: Your most effective list making will include an element of flexibility. Planning is always a process.

A family that plans together is likely to participate together. In the process of making plans, a mutuality of interest usually develops. When a parent takes time to include his children in his planning, he is in effect saying to them, "I think you are important. I want you to know what's going on in our family life and have some input into it."

Everyone wants to feel that he is part of a team, and what better team is there than one's own family? The more you develop this team feeling between members of your family, the more inclined your children will be to also redeem the time and achieve family goals.

Actually, it's not a question of whether to plan or not to plan, because making no plans is a plan in itself. If you don't redeem the time with operational goals, your dreams will become fantasies instead of realities.

If you desire more specific assistance in learning how to set personal goals, I highly recommend the

book *Strategy for Living* by Ted W. Engstrom and
Edward R. Dayton (Regal, 1981). The book deals with
goals, priorities, and planning in a practical, how-to
style.

In my own book, *The Idea Book for Mothers* (Tyn-
dale, 1981), I have included a chapter entitled "Goal-
Setting: A Statement of Faith," complete with useful
charts and worksheets.

Share Your Time. Another good way to redeem the
time is to give it away to others. Even the busiest of us
can usually find a few minutes or even an hour a day
to give to others in the form of some useful service.

There are literally hundreds of ways to share our
time.

Specifically, we all have a knack for doing something. And if we use it to serve other people, we are
giving something that no one else in the world can
give in quite the same way.

Although you may not think that what you have to
offer is valuable, it may fill a need in someone's life,
adding to his store of joy. And in these days when the
world is so full of fear, suspicion, and anxiety, joy is
one of the greatest gifts anyone can give.

So don't worry if you lack money or material things
to give to others. Of all the things a person may give,
money is probably the least permanent in the pleasure
it produces.

Instead, give yourself. This you can do extravagantly.
The gift of yourself originates from the spirit, which is
created in the image of God. The spirit, not the substance, carries the warmth that brings joy.

Here are some examples.

I once had a neighbor who read her local newspaper
for the express purpose of finding out who was admitted to the hospital. She eagerly wrote down their
names, then sent each one a cheery, "praying-for-you"

note. Doctors have told her that on several occasions her note came at just the right time; it was the turning point in strengthening someone's desire to live.

A banker who has no children of his own stops by a foster home for children one hour a week to entertain the youngsters. With each visit he imparts a fresh surge of joy and provides welcome assistance to the mother who runs the home. All with just one hour a week.

Larry is in junior high. He mows lawns for extra money. Every week, on his way home from his paying jobs, he mows the lawn of some elderly person who can't afford to pay him or of someone who is on vacation.

Norva, my daughter-in-law, thoughtfully keeps me informed about the busy doings of her and Terry, my minister son. Were it not for Norva's phone calls, much that transpires in their lives would be lost to me. Even as I am eager to hear the goings-on in their family, there are those who are interested in the happenings in your life. You can brighten their day with just a five-minute phone call.

A retired teacher goes to the local library every Tuesday evening and makes herself available to students who need assistance with their homework. A young man who had just been accepted by a state university said, "I never would have made it through school—much less prepared for college—if it hadn't been for Mrs. Stuvey."

My own mother goes to a nursing home one afternoon a week. She visits with those who have no visitors, writes letters for those who are unable to write, reads to those who can no longer see the print, and prays with those who need a fresh touch from God. All in just one afternoon a week.

Millie is a widow who visits the homes of new mothers who have no one to help them. She gives herself to these new mothers during their first two weeks at home by cleaning, washing diapers, cooking, and rocking the baby.

Becky takes time to help her three-year-old daughter, Alwyn, create handmade items for special days. She then drives Alwyn all over town to deliver her gifts. By her own unselfishness, she is teaching her daughter irreplaceable lessons about the value of giving time to others.

A Day of Rest. Another means of redeeming the time, which has blessed and benefited our family, is the observance of a day of rest.

The original day of rest was instituted in the first book of the Bible. "And on the seventh day God ended his work which he had made; and he rested on the seventh day from all his work which he had made. And God blessed the seventh day, and sanctified it: because that in it he had rested from all his work which God created and made" (Gen. 2:2, 3).

"Six days may work be done; but in the seventh is the sabbath of rest, holy to the Lord" (Exod. 31:15).

Based on the above Scriptures and others, I believe that a day of rest, one out of every seven, is a biblical principle. My purpose in mentioning the Sabbath is not to bring up theological debate about which day to keep the Sabbath or to stress the do's and don'ts of that day. My purpose is to share a miraculous happening: a day of redeemed time that has enriched our home far beyond our expectations.

As I explained in chapter 3, we hold our Sabbath dinners on Friday evenings. That marks the beginning of our day of rest. On Saturday mornings, we arise after a good night's sleep (the only day of the week that we don't set a time for rising) and frequently enjoy a sit-down breakfast with the entire family.

Then we spend several edifying, refreshing hours in

the in-depth study of God's Word, interspersed with times of prayer. Each member of the family does this alone, at his own speed.

In the late afternoon we "play" together by eating a late lunch outside or by the fireplace (depending on the weather), sharing what we've been studying, going for a walk, going to the beach, renting a movie, or reading an enjoyable book.

As I said, the results of this day have exceeded our anticipation. Our family looks forward to it every week. Bob and I don't do any money-producing work on this day, nor do we labor in the traditional sense of the word. I do my baking and cooking for this day on Friday so, aside from breakfast, we eat salads and soups. We plan to have our washing and ironing and yardwork finished by the end of the week. Often the entire household arises an hour early one day during the week to do the yardwork as a team.

When Sunday morning rolls around we are re-freshed in body and in mind as well as in spirit, ready to worship the Lord with others. By planning our day of rest as we have done, we are better able to partici-pate in this worship than had we worked all day Satur-day and awakened tired on Sunday.

Our day of rest has added physical and spiritual zest to our living. We highly recommend it.

STEWARDS OF OUR MINDS

In the beginning, a child will automatically increase his knowledge, but how much he continues to learn will depend on the amount and kind of reinforcement he gets.

For example, Scotty, a young boy who lives down the street, can make eight out of ten baskets he shoots. But it's not the score alone that counts. Does he shoot well?

In the absence of other feedback, Scotty compares himself to other children his age. Do most of them get ten baskets at a similar distance? On the basis of this information, Scotty draws conclusions about his competency.

Scotty's evaluation of himself influences his future actions. The decision that he plays basketball quite well compared to his friends motivates him to keep playing. On the other hand, Junior, who believes he plays poorly, is not motivated. So Scotty practices more than Junior and continues to improve. Junior avoids playing and looks worse as Scotty's skills increase. Their beliefs about themselves are self-fulfilling.

Mental development is self-fulfilled in the same manner.

Fay and Marijane began nursery school the same day. Prior to that day, Marijane's mother had spent much time teaching her and playing with her. Marijane could read her name, knew the basic colors, and could count to twenty.

On the opposite side of the picture, Fay had gone from one babysitter's house to another before entering nursery school. No one had really invested any quality time to expose her to specific learning skills.

In school, Marijane was quick to notice how her mental skills related to those of the other children. Though she would not be able to articulate this fact for several years to come, Marijane was beginning to conclude that she was intelligent. This conclusion influenced her motivation to learn from that time on.

In a negative sense, Fay's conclusions about herself also affected her learning ability for many years to come.

To some extent, every person's intellectual development is self-fulfilling. Each of us, consciously or not, has compared our performance to the performance of our peers. And we have used that information—

inaccurate or faulty as it might be—to draw conclusions about our mental capabilities.

If we feel good about those capabilities, we will try to improve them. But if we don't feel good about them, in all likelihood we will allow them to deteriorate. At some point, what we believe about ourselves will become a reality. If we call ourselves failures, we will tend to create a non-motivational environment for ourselves in which we feel enclosed and safe. This protective measure prevents pain and saves us from "worthless" exertion. But it also effectively seals us off from any challenge or potential enrichment.

It's true that acquiring knowledge *hurts.* It hurts mentally, and it sometimes even hurts physically. As you learn new information, you take over more and more cells in your brain. When this physical exertion becomes too heavy it's called overload, which actually causes physical discomfort—headaches, for instance, being one of the most common symptoms.

Oddly enough, there is also the *grief* that occurs when we let go of a previous understanding to embrace a new one. The longer the time between the comfort of the old state and the acceptance of the new information, the greater the emotional pain.

It's because of this that slogans such as "You can't teach an old dog new tricks" become popular. And so, many people still persuade themselves that they cannot understand mechanical things, that they have no head for science or mathematics, or that reading anything other than a newspaper or a novel is too difficult. None of this is true!

Anyone can increase his knowledge about anything if the motivation is strong enough.

My husband is a good example. He sailed in the United States Merchant Marine for several years as an able-bodied seaman. But he got so tired of sharing a room with other men on the ship that he decided to become an officer so he could enjoy a private room.

This, he realized, would entail learning to navigate, which most certainly meant becoming knowledgeable in math. As a high school student he had convinced himself that he was poor in math and could never learn higher mathematics. But eventually the desire to have a private room overcame his fear of failure, and he did learn to navigate and became an officer. What's more, he loved it.

If you have not established the habit of increasing your knowledge, you will find it difficult to begin as an adult because of the physical and emotional pain involved. To break through the barrier of non-learning, you will need a strong motive to get you moving. But if the desire is strong enough, *you can do it!*

Writing is difficult for me. It hurts. The immediate motive is never the same when I undertake a writing project. I have written because it was an outlet for praising the Lord. I have written because I believed that I had something very significant to share. I have written because I needed the money. And I have written on occasion to influence the public. But each time I have undertaken a writing project, the motive had to be stronger than the struggle. It had to provide a reward that would be greater than the pain.

Motivate Your Child to Learn. I encourage parents to *use every positive motivational force available* to develop habits of intellectual achievement in their children.

It's these developed habits that give endurance during the long, difficult times. In everyone's life, there will come "dry spells" when it's hard to get going and doing. That's why it's important for children to develop positive habits early in life.

Motivating children to learn can take several forms. Some of the methods we used were these:

1. Offering money for reading books. (We determined the amount according to the book's difficulty or the importance of its moral.)

2. Joining good quality book clubs.

3. Subscribing to mind-stretching magazines.

4. Taking regular trips to museums and libraries.

5. Vacationing in places of historic and geographical significance.

6. Hosting missionaries in our home during church missions conferences.

7. Inviting foreign exchange students into our home for several months at a time.

You can create other motivational activities to fit your circumstances and family.

Overall, I believe one of the best motivations for children is an exemplary parental example. We as parents should develop our minds, if for no other reason, because God desires us to do so. The Bible says, "God hath not given us the spirit of fear; but of power, and of love, and of a sound mind" (2 Tim. 1:7). When we develop the sound mind God has given us, we bring glory to God.

God expects us to renew our minds (Rom. 12:2) and use them to study to show ourselves approved unto him (2 Tim. 2:15). When it comes to grasping biblical truths, it is essential that we learn to stretch our minds. We acquire God's eternal truths in exactly the same way we acquire any other knowledge. It takes the same physical and emotional pain. There are no shortcuts. But it is never too late to learn.

We don't need to be like the Corinthians whom Paul admonished because they were too lazy to discipline their minds to "bring into captivity every thought" in order for them to be able to receive the strong meat of the Word (1 Cor. 3:2; 2 Cor. 10:5). We can always change the seeds we plant in our minds in order to bring forth a new harvest.

How? What should we feed our minds to increase our knowledge and ability to learn? The following intellectual diet has helped both myself and my husband. You could probably add to the list.

Avoid TV. When you habitually feed on TV fare, you are allowing ungodly minds to shape both your thinking and your store of knowledge. Also, the more TV you watch, the more difficult it will be for you to discipline your mind to concentrated reading and study, even of God's Word.

Instead, read beneficial books. Read widely. Encourage your children to read history and historical fiction. Make the reading of biographies a high priority, especially those of famous men and women of achievement and godly men and women. Read books about travel and books set in other geographical locations. Read books about the Bible. But more importantly, *read the Bible.* Provide a model for your child by reading and knowing the Bible yourself.

Visit museums and art galleries, then obtain books to read about their offerings. Seek out the company of thinking people, people with ideas and high aspirations. Expose your children to these people in your home.

Indoctrinate your children into the joys of reading, thinking, and meditating in a quiet and peaceful atmosphere, without the deleterious effects of loud background music. Teach your children the hypnotic dangers of video games which, like TV, discourage thinking and bend and shape the mind. They may increase hand-eye coordination, but what a cost!

With God's help, we can all become good stewards of our money, our time, and our minds—and show our children how to do the same.

6: HOW TO REAP A PEACEFUL SPIRIT

Our home was full of young people that night of the annual Christmas party, and during a lull in activity, I exulted in the harvest around me. It was a harvest of youth from months of weekly Bible studies. I studied the four grouped by the hot cider bowl.

There was Pete: gregarious, outwardly alive with the Spirit, overtly praising God in word and song. Yet for nearly two years he had evidenced a constant unsettledness, often marked by periods of deep gloom and depression.

Phyllis had made tremendous spiritual progress, attested to by her growing familiarity with the Word. In keeping with her new perception of God's love, she had begun to dress and fix herself prettier. However, I could not help but notice her struggle to look and sound enthusiastic.

Katie's growth expressed itself in her quiet self-assurance. But Bill was another story altogether.

Each and every week during the year, Bill had been glum and depressed when he arrived at our home. By the time the worship and Bible study concluded, he was excited again about life in general and his possibilities in Christ in particular. But the next week, he would be back at square one.

Throughout the past year, Bob and I had spent quite a bit of time with these young people. Each of them had been exposed to approximately the same opportunities for growth. Yet all had not made equal advances.

What, I asked myself, caused the difference? As I pondered the question, the homes of each of the four flashed across the screen of my mind.

Pete's parents are professional people who are never at home except to sleep. Their home is cluttered, and it seems as though no one ever has time to look at the piles of things collecting dust.

Phyllis's home is so heavily curtained and locked that it is oppressive. One can hardly conduct a conversation above the sound of either the furnace or air conditioner blowing dry air around. Phyllis's mother never sees beyond today.

Katie's parents are retired missionaries—soft-spoken, gentle people. Everything about their persons and home is quiet and serene. Their door is always open to help others.

Bill's home is filled with music, usually rock, blasting at full volume. Bill's father doesn't live there—only Bill and his constantly bickering mother and grandfather.

Immediately, I had my answer. It was one of God's natural laws: We prepare the soil for future plantings.

The soil, or ambience, of each of these Christian homes was responsible for both the amount and quality of spiritual nutrients it imparted to its residents.

A CHRISTIAN HOME

We often talk about the importance of a Christian home. And yet, what is a Christian home? It's a place where Christ is honored. Yes, we would all agree on that. Naturally, it's a place where prayers are said. We would also agree that it's a place where the Bible is frequently or regularly read. And, of course, it's a place where the peace of God resides. Well . . . maybe . . . well, at least sometimes.

If peace is one of the qualities that should characterize a Christian home, what, exactly, does the word mean?

Webster gives us these synonyms: quiet, tranquility, harmony, order. We'll examine the meanings of these four words one at a time.

In our examination, we will be discussing some rather unusual topics. The subject of Christian homes is ordinarily couched in biblical or theological terms. These terms do provide valid descriptions to use as models for our homes.

However, I believe there are other frames of reference that could and should be raised in discussing Christian homes. For I am convinced that certain elements of today's society have invaded our households with numerous disruptive forces that mitigate against peaceful living.

These invasions have been so subtle, so illusory, and yet so destructive, that they have shipwrecked myriads of families, *without those families even being aware of how it all came about!*

As a result, "for lack of knowledge," as Hosea 4:6 tells us, God's people are perishing. If this is true, as it appears to be, then obviously something must be done about it.

Let's begin by looking at Webster's first synonym for peace.

QUIET

What is *quiet?* My young neighbor's definition is simply "not noisy." A very good definition.

When William H. Stewart, M.D., was the surgeon general of the United States, he made a most amazing statement on the subject. He said, "Calling noise a nuisance is like calling smog an inconvenience. Noise must be considered a hazard to the health of people everywhere." With these words, Stewart placed noise in the same category as a virus—something to be controlled and, where possible, eliminated.

But just how noisy is noise? The chart in this chapter provides comparative points of reference to help you determine your own home's noise level.

SOUND LEVEL CHART

0 — Threshold of audibility
10 — Barely detectable
20
30 — Audible whisper
40
45 — Hushed residence
50
60 — Moderated conversation
— Air conditioner
65 — Annoying
70 — Fairly loud speech
— Television audio
74 — Vacuum cleaner
75 — Dishwasher
78 — Clothes washer

80 — Intolerable for telephone use
  — Loud singing
  — Garbage disposal
85 — Ear damage possible
88 — Food blender
90 — Speech interference
  — Shouting
96 — Power mower
100 — Heat furnace
105 — Motorcycle
110 — Baby's screaming
115 — Maximum under federal law
118 — Chain saw
120
130
140 — Pain threshold
150
160
163 — Toy cap pistol

The chart shows that environmental noise affects us in two ways: first, with annoyance; second, with actual physical damage.

Upon his return from an around-the-world sabbatical trip, the minister of a large California church was asked, "What were the most interesting sights or experiences you encountered?"

After Earl Lee's glowing answer to that question, he was asked, "What was the most disturbing element of your trip?"

Without a pause, the pastor answered, "Pollution."

"What kind of pollution?"

"All kinds. But especially *noise pollution.*"

Lee's observation agrees with that of many medical doctors and researchers, who say that annoyance or stress induced by noise is responsible for numerous physical reactions. For example, when we are exposed to certain levels of noise any or all of the following physical reactions might occur: blood vessels constrict, giving rise to increased blood pressure; heart rate increases; muscles become tense; perspiration tends to increase; adrenaline output rises markedly; kidneys become more active; liver function changes measurably; the pupils of the eye dilate; breathing rate increases; and brain chemistry changes may occur.

The body reacts generally to noise, contributing to feelings of fatigue, irritability, or tension. Other bodily reactions to noise include even digestive system upsets, which in some cases lead to the formation of stress ulcers.

Rosie's case is a graphic example of these effects. Even as a child Rosie had never been free of stomach pain. As she grew older, her painful stomach attacks became more severe until one night she began vomiting blood. Doubled up in agony, Rosie was rushed to the emergency room, where she was treated for a perforated stomach ulcer.

After successful surgery, the doctor queried Rosie about the stress and noise level of her home over the past years.

Rosie admitted, "My parents were always shouting at each other and at us kids."

"Did it bother you?"

She thought a moment, then shrugged. "I learned to not consciously hear it."

A much-quoted warning that bears repeating is from Samuel Rosen, M.D., of the New York Mount Sinai Hospital: "You may learn to ignore noise, but your body will never forgive you!"

Jack Westman, a psychiatrist at the University of Wisconsin, speaks to the disruptive influence of noise in the home. *"Togetherness at the supper table is hampered by household noises and by the general tenseness fanned by the daylong din . . . ,"* he said. "We don't understand that noise makes us less efficient, less effective, and more tense. Instead, we scapegoat. We take our tensions out on each other. Mothers yell at the youngsters. Parents bicker."

When this happens, children sadly begin to equate noise with attention.

One day I heard a neighbor criticizing her children for arguing so loudly. "Why can't you ever play together peacefully?" she screamed at them. Following her mother's example, tiny Lorie shouted back, "You'd never notice us if we did."

At one time, the home was considered to be a man's castle, his haven from the noise and bustle, from the stress-producing elements of the world. But with the introduction of a growing list of noise-producing devices into the family environment, this is no longer the case.

With our selection of lawn mowers, snowblowers, chain saws, blenders, sink disposals, garbage compacters, clothes washers and dryers, doorbells, plumbing noises, and central heating and air-conditioning, noise pollution presently appears to be outstripping air pollution.

In addition to the common household noises just described, a majority of children are now matter-of-factly exposed to such familiar toys as firecrackers and cap pistols, along with an alarming proliferation of noisy, battery-operated toys and video games.

Clearly, in our age of electronic gadgetry, noisy tools, appliances, toys, and home equipment will continue to increase. So instead of wishing it would all go away—which it won't—homemakers must combat noise pollution.

How to Prevent Noise Pollution. Though in some cases industry has made great strides in eliminating noise pollution, little has been done to address the problem in many homes. Yet it is possible, even without the expenditure of huge sums of money, to control, minimize, and in some areas, even eliminate excess noise in our homes. Let me make a few suggestions.

Wooden stairs can become a source of frequent, irritating noise, especially when often used by children. If the cost of covering them with wall-to-wall carpet is beyond one's budget, there are alternatives—carpet runners, for example. When our children were small, even the cost of runners was unaffordable. So I went to several carpet stores, purchased a number of last year's samples at a considerable savings, and tacked these onto the stairs. Our children all enjoyed the colorful stairway.

Jangling telephone bells are an irritation I can well do without. I learned that this noise can be corrected on most telephones by simply adjusting the volume control on the base of the machine. If the bell is still too loud, some telephone vendors provide a soft-toned replacement bell.

Kitchen noises tend to wear on women who spend several hours a day in this room. Many of these sounds can be softened or eliminated by the use of pads and mats. For example, a thick foam rubber mat underneath blenders and mixers is an effective deterrent to their usual high pitch. Pads strategically placed on work surfaces also help eliminate the clang and clatter of pots and pans. Cork tile glued to the shelves and backs of cupboards reduces dish racket. Replacing old or worn cupboard door latches with quiet-closing magnetic latches removes another sound.

Often a child will run in and out of his house slamming doors behind him. Parents who shout, "Come back and close that door quietly!" only further add to the din. As soon as a child can reach a door handle, he should be taught to open and close doors by *turning the handle,* not by slamming the door. He will remember to do this more easily if he has good models. You might also consider installing automatic door closers on outside screen doors.

Dishwashers and clothes washers need not be started while people are in adjacent rooms; they can be turned on after people have left the area. I also find it a good idea to do noisy chores such as vacuuming in the early morning when I feel refreshed by a good night's sleep. I have learned that I am better able to resist stress-producing noises at that time of day.

Because basements are normally constructed of solid-surface foundation materials such as cinder blocks or poured concrete, they tend to be quite reverberant. And unless the basement is to be used as a living area, the cost of paneling is often prohibitive. I solved this problem in one home in which we lived by purchasing some end-of-the-roll carpet and gluing it on the wall. In addition to eliminating noise, this innovation proved to be attractive and inexpensive as well.

For some families, a major source of conflict is the use of entertainment equipment, specifically, radios, televisions, phonographs, and musical instruments. Of course, headsets are for some an adequate solution to the problem. However, headsets also pose a potential problem to the listener: Unmonitored high noise levels can result in severe and permanent ear damage. Furthermore, if a child uses headsets on a regular basis, parents tend to pay little attention to his choice of music. For these reasons, I personally discourage parents from allowing their children to use headsets.

Clyde Narramore, an eminent Christian psychologist, suggests an alternative. He once wrote a booklet extolling the value of filling your home with classical and praise music. He is right. These kinds of music will provide a serene, uplifting atmosphere to your home. On the other hand, the all too common rock music, to which millions of people have become addicted, not only destroys the peace and quiet of a home, but creates jangled nerves, high blood pressure, and a host of other physical and mental disturbances.

Noise—any and all kinds—will not just go away if you ignore it. Only concentrated efforts will result in its elimination or control. But simple as it may sound, *one of the best ways to reduce noise from your home or surroundings is to not make it in the first place.* To do that, consider implementing some of the following suggestions:

1. Use plastic trash baskets and garbage cans. They're much quieter than metal containers and often cost less, too.

2. Train yourself and your children *not to shout messages or requests from room to room.* It's very annoying to the other family members who aren't involved in the conversation.

3. Learn to walk lightly and train your children to do the same. Don't allow indiscriminate running in the house.

4. When removing your shoes, slip out of them. Don't drop them on the floor.

5. If you have dogs, train them not to bark indiscriminately. The barking of dogs definitely exceeds the annoyance level.

6. When moving or rearranging furniture, don't slide or drag it across the room. Lift it if at all possible.

7. Isolate the television to a single room where the noise does not reverberate. Then *keep the volume turned down.*

8. If you or your children use a clock-radio alarm, be sure to preset and pretest the volume level the night before its use to prevent a sudden blast of morning wakeup music.

9. If possible, schedule your lawn-mowing chores at times when the noise will provide the least annoyance to others.

My husband recalls an afternoon in the home of a California businessman that was one of the most restful visits of his life. Though the business was new and the family wasn't very affluent, he was aware of a peaceful atmosphere from the moment he stepped in the front door.

"Soft, tasteful music was playing on the record player," he told me, "and the three small children, though very active, were soft-spoken and respectful." He heard not a single jangling noise or raised voice during his time there. "Those few hours instilled in me the conviction that it is possible for families with children to *live* in a quietly moderated atmosphere."

It is not beyond the realm of possibility for each family to realize such a goal.

TRANQUILITY

This second synonym for *peace* means "free from emotional disturbances or agitation." Noise, of course, produces emotional disturbances and agitation. However, other, more subtle forces can also cause physical or mental distress. The following illustration highlights one of them.

Two Christian couples, married the same day, chose two different locales for their honeymoon trip. The DeWitts decided to spend their first two weeks of wedded bliss at America's most traditional honeymoon site: Niagara Falls. The Tolsons opted for Israel, which they believed would be an ideal, spiritually meaningful place in which to begin their lives together.

Later, when they compared notes, some interesting and puzzling facts came to light. First, as the DeWitts had expected, Niagara Falls proved to be the exhilarating honeymoon spot they had anticipated.

"We had a *wonderful* time!" they exclaimed. "How about your trip to Israel? Was it all you'd hoped for?"

The Tolsons looked at each other. Jack shook his

head. "I don't understand it. Everything should have been perfect. . . . It was the dream of both of us to visit 'God's Land' . . . but we were miserable the whole time."

"Miserable?" Shirley DeWitt exclaimed. "How could that be?"

Gwen Tolson shook her head. "We quarreled every day—something we'd never done before. It was awful."

"I'm sorry," Duane DeWitt said. "But I don't understand."

Jack sighed, "Neither do we, for we've been doing fine since returning home."

How could this be? Were the non-quarreling DeWitts more spiritual than the Tolsons?

Actually, both couples were greatly affected by an intangible condition in the air known as the ion balance or ion effect.

As is the case with all matter, the air is made up of molecules that have an electrical charge. Scientists define this charge as *ionization*. Studies have proven that when there is an imbalance of either positive or negative charges (ions) in the air, the health of all life is affected.

More than five thousand scientific documents in several languages report experiments that support this general conclusion: An overdose of positive ions is bad for you; an overload of negative ions is beneficial. If the air is charged with too many positive ions, life becomes uncomfortable for everyone—insufferable for some. But an overdose of negative ions in the air invariably produces a gloriously tranquilizing effect that eases tension and leaves us full of energy.

Since moving water releases a lot of negative ions into the air, Niagara Falls is one of the greatest negative ion generators in the whole world—the reason for the marvelous sense of well-being the DeWitts experienced.

On the other hand, the Tolsons visited Israel during the time of the desert wind called the *Sharav*. While the *Sharav* blows, for days and often weeks, it tips the ion balance in the air to the positive side.

The Tolsons' irritability was not at all unusual. Israeli doctors blame the desert wind for a long list of increased physical discomforts such as sleeplessness, irritability, pain around the heart, headaches, difficulty in breathing, and irrational tension and anxiety.

Felix Sulman and his team of scientists at the School of Applied Pharmacology in Jerusalem have produced evidence that the ion balance in the air we breathe—not just in Israel or Niagara Falls, but anywhere we might live—is critical to our physical and emotional well-being.

Albert P. Krueger, an American microbiologist and experimental pathologist, confirmed Sulman's Jerusalem research. As he was working with bacteria that float in the air and spread diseases—mostly colds, influenza, and other respiratory ills—Krueger found that an astonishingly small quantity of negative ions could kill those bacteria quickly.

While he was chairman of the Department of Bacteriology at the University of California at Berkeley, Krueger published his findings. He stated that an excess of positive ions caused hyperactivity in mammals, which could lead rapidly to exhaustion, anxiety, and possibly, depression. Rabbits, for instance, one of the most timid of all creatures, behave aggressively when they receive an overdose of positive ions. Krueger also said that an excess of negative ions seemed to have a calming effect, able to counteract a positive ion overdose and generally duplicate the effect of the common tranquilizer.

Almost everyone has experienced the mild shock that occurs, especially during dry weather, when one walks briskly through a carpeted room and then touches another person or a piece of metal such as a doorknob. This static electricity is caused by friction between a negative and a positive charge—in this case, friction generated by walking on a carpet.

But static electricity also happens when we wear clothes that are totally or partially made from synthetic fabrics. These clothes may cling to us or release sparks when we take them off. Why?

Synthetic fabrics possess a positive potential. In other words, when they encounter friction, they generate a positive charge and give off positive ions. Only fabric made from cotton has neither a positive nor a negative potential. However, other natural fibers such as wool or silk carry negligible charges.

The synthetic clothing we wear is not the only carrier of positive ions. Heating and air-conditioning are also culprits. Most of the air that is forced from either of these systems into our rooms and cars is likely to be overloaded with positive ions.

Asthmatics and other people with respiratory problems often suffer additional agonies from positive charges in the air and in clothes. The rest of us are usually unaware of any of the effects from these sources. At times we may simply find ourselves restive, irritable, or just not up-to-par for seemingly no reason at all.

Beverly, for example, was a healthy child. But when she turned fourteen and started junior high school, she suddenly began experiencing headaches. These became increasingly severe until they developed into full-fledged migraines. The girl was examined by doctors who found nothing wrong and pronounced her psychosomatic. She was prayed over, and she begged God to heal her.

Finally, the parents realized that Beverly's problems all began when she started wearing nylon underclothing like the other junior high girls. At approximately the same time, Beverly's parents had redone her room with frilly curtains, bedspread, and canopy—all made from a synthetic material.

For Bev, the additional positive ions created by close contact with so many synthetic materials was enough to throw her body chemistry off-balance. But when the synthetic clothing and bedroom fabrics were replaced with natural fabrics, the girl's headaches immediately disappeared.

The Ion Effect in Your Home. How can we best develop a proper ion balance in our homes so as to minimize unnecessary physical and emotional disturbances? There are a number of helpful things you can do.

First, read books about the ion effect. This will give you a fuller understanding of the important part ions play in our health. These books will also provide you with additional guidelines and ideas.

Second, at least until you are better informed on the subject, curtail the purchase and wearing of synthetic materials as much as possible. Instead, use natural fabrics such as cotton, linen, silk, and wool. If you are unable to purchase fabrics that are one hundred percent natural, try to find those that have a significant amount of natural fibers in them. Even though some of these fabrics have to be ironed, you will find in time that the benefits are worth the extra care effort.

Third, if you suspect a heavy positive ion concentration in the air, shower frequently. Remember, moving water generates many negative ions.

Fourth, place living plants in every room possible. Plants are nature's most prolific source of negative ions. In operation, plants extract the negative energy from the earth and eject it from the tips of their leaves. This scientific principle was discovered and reported by Christian Bach.

I discovered the value of indoor plants quite by

accident, long before I knew anything about ions or the ion effect. Since flowers often winter-killed in Michigan, where I lived at the time, I decided to save some of my yard flowers by moving them into the house.

So I filled several wash tubs with dirt and had my boys carry them upstairs to my bedroom. Then I transplanted my lovely flowers from the yard into these containers. From that time on, throughout the winter months, whenever one entered the room he invariably experienced an uplifting, almost euphoric sense of well-being. You can well imagine that this room soon became the most popular one in the house.

I often noticed that I felt revived and ready-to-go again after spending time in my room. I then thought my refreshed spirits had something to do with the cheery atmosphere wrought by the bright little flowers. I know now that it had more to do with the strong negative ion count they produced.

HARMONY

Now that we've learned how to produce quiet, healthful environments in our homes, let's examine another synonym for peace: harmony.

Our perception of harmony in a place, including a home, begins with light and color. Life as we know it is sustained by light. People and all living creatures survive thanks to the energy of sunlight.

God has many things to say about light. Among them, perhaps one of the most important, is this: "Light is come into the world, and men loved darkness rather than light, because their deeds were evil. For every one that doeth evil hateth the light, neither cometh to the light, lest his deeds should be reproved" (John 3:19, 20). *Light uncovers evil.*

Personally, I believe this statement is literally true.

So if you want a home that's in agreement with God's Word, you must fill it with light. Flood it with as much natural sunlight as possible and the best artificial lighting you can find.

Poorly lit rooms encourage disobedience and sloppy living habits, whereas well-lit rooms encourage discipline and cleanliness. Children raised in homes with dim lighting rarely learn to read quickly or well. And it is a statistical fact that the installation of good lighting in high-crime areas immediately lowers the crime rate.

The Effects of Color. The effects of light and color go hand in hand. Many parents paint rooms or buy clothes for their children in colors that please themselves, not realizing the negative impact these colors could have on other members of the family.

My friend Sheri learned firsthand the influence of color upon a child. Sheri's daughter, Sara, had a lengthy, complicated birth. The birth difficulties affected Sara's motor responses to the degree that, when she learned to walk, she had a tendency to fall unexpectedly.

When the child was old enough to be taken to the park, Sheri always clothed her in red to be able to spot her more readily if she fell. The frequency of Sara's falls at the park increased so dramatically that a doctor was consulted.

The doctor told my friend that conditions such as Sara's could sometimes be diminished in both frequency and severity if the patient was protected against red or yellow colors. He also told Sheri to give the child glasses with green lenses, which she did. The improvement was incredible.

For some reason, red seems to exert stimulating influence, while green does just the opposite. I used to think these were merely learned responses until

I took time to read scientific case studies on the subject.

In one case study, mink were reared behind different colored plastic windows. Mink are ordinarily quite vicious, particularly during the mating period. In the test, mink that were kept behind pink plastic became increasingly aggressive.

On the other hand, mink kept behind blue plastic became more docile and could be handled like house pets. It was evident that the mink were excited by red radiation and pacified by blue radiation.

In experiments with infants, who obviously have no prior experience with color, blue light tends to lessen activity and crying. This reinforces the fact that our reactions to color as adults are not due solely to cultural training.

Various responses to color have also been observed in blindfolded subjects, suggesting that human reactions to color are not entirely conscious. Even conditions of tension and relaxation are noticeably affected by color.

Color and light directly affect our level of activity. When either children or adults are exposed to illumination with warm colors—such as yellow, peach, or pink—they are generally more cheerful, alert, and active. This should be remembered when decorating living areas where manual tasks are performed or physical activity engaged in—kitchens, dining rooms, playrooms, bathrooms, and family rooms.

Color and light also affect one's ability to concentrate. With this in mind, use cooler hues such as gray, blue, green, or turquoise to produce quieter surroundings. These combinations produce little distraction, which enables people to better concentrate on difficult visual and mental tasks. Cool colors are ideal for study rooms, libraries, bedrooms, offices, and formal living rooms.

Parents who understand the effects of color can

often lessen and even eliminate hyperactivity in their children—or encourage increased activity in passive children.

Color also affects our body temperature. As a child, I grew up in homes that my mother painted white throughout. She used colors only to trim and accent. I remember that guests who entered our homes often would comment, "How cool it seems in here." At the time, I never connected those comments with the color of the rooms. Following my mother's example, when I married I also used colors as she had.

Not until I began studying color and its effects did I note some interesting facts. My mother is usually physically very warm, while I am usually physically cool. The color schemes my mother habitually chose tended to enhance her well-being, but had just the opposite effect on me. They made me feel cold all the time.

The following color "temperature values" will provide you with a brief decorating-for-harmony guide.

White is notorious for making one feel cool. The same is true of blues and greens. This means that you could practically air-condition a house for the price of a few cans of blue, green, or white paint—well, at least these colors would make you feel air-conditioned.

Mixing white or blue with another color also creates a cool cast. Lavender, for example, is a cold color since it is purple combined with white and blue.

At the other end of the thermal palette are the deep, warm colors, the "wood-and-fireplace" colors that tend to take the chill out of an environment. These include all colors that approach yellow or red in their tone. Even blue and white become warmer in tone when they are mixed with yellow. Greens are cold as they approach blue, but warm as they approach yellow. Purple colors increase in warmth as the ratio of red to blue in them increases.

Learning to gauge the "temperature" of colors will help you decorate in a way that will enhance your home life. For those who are interested in learning more about color, there are many helpful books in most libraries.

ORDER

Our final synonym for peace, *order,* has a marked effect upon our homes. According to Webster, order is "a fixed or definite plan." It also means "to regulate; to manage."

God is a God of order. If there is no orderliness in our homes, how can we expect him to live there?

Though the Bible teaches that the man is primarily responsible for the spiritual climate of the family, the woman is primarily responsible for the home. This is clearly indicated in Proverbs 31:10–31, which describes a God-honoring woman. Every woman today ought to study this Scripture until it becomes so much a part of her that it directly influences her behavior. Because, among other attributes, the woman described here has a definite plan by which she wisely and skillfully regulates her household.

She is trustworthy. She clothes her family well. She is ambitious. She purchases the best food possible and sees to it that every person in her house eats properly. She develops business skills. She takes care of herself physically. And she does not give in to lazy desires of the flesh.

This godly woman maintains good work habits and is unselfish. She provides for her own family *and* gives to the poor and needy as well. She prepares herself for any situation, keeps herself attractive, develops her creative skills, and markets the fruit thereof. Furthermore, in the midst of all this organization and activity, *she keeps control of her tongue.*

To sum up her attributes and accomplishments: She brings effective order and leadership to her home—the place where the *shalom* (peace) of God dwells.

In Proverbs 31:23 we read, "Her husband is known in the gates, when he sitteth among the elders of the land." This does not mean that the man of the family loafs around at the coffee shop. It *does* mean that the order in the home of the woman under discussion is so complete that her husband is respected in the community as a godly man and as such, has earned the privilege to give godly advice to others.

Without a doubt, the godly woman described in Proverbs 31 was a model to her own community. She's a model to us as well.

A friend of mine whose cousin Francis competed in the Mrs. America contest told me this story.

Francis and another woman were the finalists. Up to this point it had appeared that the two were on par in practically every area. "The item that tipped the scales in favor of the other contestant," Francis said, "was the atmosphere in her home. It had something I couldn't duplicate. . . ."

Even though Francis's family was on its best behavior, they were unable to create the serene atmosphere that seemed to come so naturally to her opponent's family. The daily life in Francis's home had always been noisy and unstructured. Thus, even for this important occasion, the family was unable to simulate a peaceful ambience. They tried, but failed.

Though it came too late to make a difference in this situation, Francis had learned an important lesson: Her children would not convey a peaceful spirit unless she planted its seeds by creating a peaceful home.

One day our side door opened and Larry, one of the college students who attends our Bible study, came rushing into the house and sat down in the living room. When I walked in and greeted him he said,

"Please, may I sit here awhile? I've just got to soak up some of this peace."

The peace Larry wanted to soak up was the presence of God. A home that radiates peace always announces the presence of God to those who enter its portals. One of the barometers I watch for in my home is how long it has been since someone stated, "How peaceful it is here."

For if others aren't able to discern a definite, peaceful ambience in my home, I need to start checking my personal spiritual aptitude and the condition of my physical surroundings. The consequences affect not only my spirit, but also those of everyone around me.

7: HOW TO REAP A POSITIVE SELF-IMAGE

Marion and I were both speakers at a seminar in Chicago. We had known each other just a few months, and this was our first time to work together. Marion was nervous at breakfast, though I thought little of it. But when she got up to speak, I could scarcely believe what I was seeing.

Marion was visibly shaking when she walked to the podium. Then, as she spoke, she actually *read* her paper word for word, making no eye contact with her listeners. In other circumstances, it might not have been so bad, but this was a seminar geared to teach women to become more self-confident.

As Marion spoke, I watched the women's reactions. Having heard of Marion's qualifications, they were eager and expectant—at first. But within a few minutes, first one woman, then another, laid down her pen and stopped taking notes. I couldn't blame them, because Marion was not communicating effectively.

Afterwards, when I spoke to her, I said, "You do know your subject, but. . . ."

She began to cry.

"I know I did everything wrong," she said. "And I was afraid to look at the ladies. I didn't think I *looked* qualified. . . . I didn't think anyone would want to listen to me."

During the ensuing conversation Marion told me how her father had always criticized her desire to make herself look nice. "It's vain and sinful to seek a mirror's approval," he told her. "That's exalting one's image, and God hates that."

The key word was *image*—not so much the mirror's image, but Marion's self-image. Marion's picture of herself was so poor that she had avoided looking the women at the seminar in the eye, for fear of their criticism.

The word *image* makes many people uncomfortable. Marion's father was one of them. It is true that God told us not to bow down to images. Marion's father interpreted this commandment to mean that if one spent time on his or her appearance, it would displease God.

To others, the word conveys another negative meaning: "sham or cover-up," connoting an attempt to conceal one's real self, especially the flaws he might possess.

Webster's dictionary defines image as "a tangible or visible representation" of something. In line with this definition, God told his people in Exodus 20:3–5 not to make a tangible representation of anything for the purpose of worshiping it.

By image in this discussion, we mean public image,

which is totally different than the definition used in Exodus. A public image should be an accurate replication of a person, as true as one's image in the mirror. In seeking to create a good public image, we actually focus on how to become the people God intended us to be.

Some people say we shouldn't care what others think of our image. Personally, *I care* about the image I portray because I represent Jesus, the Son of the living God. If I present a poor image to the people around me, I am encouraging them to pass wrong judgment on the God I serve.

FIRST IMPRESSIONS

We have heard it said, "You never have a second chance to make a good first impression." That's generally true.

The initial impression you make on people, whether good or bad, always has to do with the way you dress and the way you behave—in other words, the image you project.

If people have no other measuring stick with which to judge you, your appearance and behavior will be their guide. So you can do yourself a favor, and at the same time, create an interest in the God you serve, by communicating a positive image.

First contacts with other people are usually brief, which give us only a momentary opportunity to tell them who we are. That means we must make an instant statement if we're going to make one at all.

So our clothing often makes that statement for us. Of all the personality "signals" people in our society transmit to the world, one of the strongest is clothing. Every time you dress, you make choices about the way you want to appear, the statement you want to convey. Your clothes can say, "Hey, I feel good about who I am!" Or, all too often, reveal, "I'm not so sure about myself." Even "I-don't-care" attire shouts a clear message to that effect.

Many people dress to gain acceptance, or to identify with a particular group. Some dress to protest or to emulate, others to attract or to intimidate. And thousands of people of all ages seem to be so frustrated by their inability to communicate that they frequently resort to "message" T-shirts.

Some youth aptly use clothing to derive pleasure or power from the negative attention it attracts. For example, a girl wears a man's oversized green plaid shirt as a dress, and an unshaven boy dons a psychedelic T-shirt. These teenagers are not concerned with gaining your approval. Their intent is simply to invade your space, to force your attention to them, and thus, to manipulate your behavior. They nearly always achieve their objective.

We can rejoice that each of us is unique. A thread of individual identity is woven throughout the fabric of each of our lives. But it's important that we use this gift to bring glory to our heavenly Father instead of simply using it to draw attention to ourselves.

When we express our individuality by appearing in public either poorly or wrongly dressed, we naturally receive negative attention. Unfortunately, this attention not only reflects poorly on our Creator, but also on ourselves. Over time, the negative reactions of others can produce chronic feelings of inferiority and inadequacy in us.

There is a distinct cycle. The way you feel about yourself often dictates the way you are treated. For instance, if on a particular day you feel especially good about yourself and dress accordingly, you will receive special treatment from your fellow employees, your family, *and* public servants. Try this for yourself and see if it isn't true.

On the other hand, if you feel decidedly unworthy or

dejected, and your dress expresses that fact, you will quickly note the difference in the treatment you receive.

By altering the impression your clothes make, you will set off a whole series of changes in people's responses to you. Conversely, as people respond differently to you—positively *or* negatively—your feelings about yourself will change.

What Do My Clothes Say? One way to learn what you are communicating to others by the way you look is to play a game that we call, "What Do My Clothes Say?" Each of us reacts—either consciously or unconsciously—to the way other people are dressed. Typically, we are not prone to express our feelings aloud, but this game gives you the opportunity to do so.

The rules for "What Do My Clothes Say?" are simple. Point to an article of clothing worn by one of the players, and ask a question or make a statement.

For example, I point to my freshly starched white blouse and ask my three-year-old son, "What does my blouse say?" (I think it is telling him I want to look fresh and nice for him.)

He answers, "It says, 'Don't hug me.' "

I point to his T-shirt, which he has put on wrong-side out and backwards. "Your shirt tells me you were in a hurry to get dressed, so you were careless."

"No, Mother," he says. "It's supposed to tell you that I'm a ballplayer, and this"—he points to the size 6 label—"is my number."

Do you get the idea? The game can be very revealing.

Clearly, other people don't always see us the way we intend them to. As your child grows older, this concept will help him accept the importance of good grooming and can ease some of the strain that often arises over clothing during a child's teenage years.

I know a first-grade teacher who used this game in his classroom. He told me, "One of the problems we often face in school is that some children tend to ostracize others for no other reason than the way they dress."

"Has this game helped solve the problem?" I asked him.

"Definitely. In a very short time it promoted better understanding among the children."

YOUR CLOTHES MAKE A DIFFERENCE

The clothing you wear affects your mood at least as much as it affects other's attitudes toward you. Check this out for yourself. You'll find that when you wear casual clothes, even your spoken language tends to become more casual.

Here's a test you can take. The next rainy Saturday afternoon, stay at home to catch up on your letter writing. First, bundle yourself up in that old, worn bathrobe. Write a letter or two, then get up, take a shower, don a cheery dress, and finish your letter writing.

You will notice a different tone in the letters you wrote when you were attired attractively. The people who receive your letters may never know what you wore when you wrote them, but they will certainly be affected by the tone of the contents.

Of course, your child's mood is also greatly affected by the clothing he wears. Suppose one afternoon you both decide to paint a picture. When you and your child are wearing crisp, clean shirts, your painting will reflect a different mood than when you are both still dragging around in pajamas.

This principle explains why the behavior of people when they're dressed up sometimes differs from their normal conduct. Their state of mind is conditioned by the awareness of their special appearance.

So if you are feeling down and depressed, don't succumb to the temptation to dress in old, dreary clothes. Put on the brightest, most colorful clothes you have. Your spirits will soon reflect what you are wearing.

Sick or bedridden patients also should be encouraged to wear nice gowns or pajamas. Feeling good about how you look, even when you're ill, helps ward off depression. And depression, as many doctors now think, lowers the body's ability to fight disease. According to an article in *USA Today*, two New York psychiatrists have proven what so many have already suspected. "We don't know exactly what's going on," said Steven Schleifer, one of the researchers, "but it's clear, depression can lower the body's immune functions."

All the more reason for any person—and especially sick or weary ones—to dress nicely.

Clothing also can be a positive protection for fragile egos, a personality booster for the insecure. For that reason, one must look his or her best when interviewing for a new job, when beginning school, when going on that first date, when expecting the pastor for dinner.

This points out a well-founded reason why some schools require their students to wear uniforms. Uniforms speak a universal language around the world, often imbuing the wearer with a rank and authority he would not otherwise possess. For some children this is very beneficial.

There was a time in my youngest son's teenage life when he didn't feel very good about himself. During this time, David's strong desire to dress in the fashion of his school peers greatly increased. This change in dress was altering his personality in a negative way.

Bob and I made the decision to place him in the military academy. One of the immediate benefits was that the uniform he wore gave a boost to his self-esteem. Free from the constant worry of how he looked to his peers—all the cadets wore the same uniform—he could move with greater confidence. This new assurance began to reverse his previous lack of interest in academic growth.

An additional benefit was the colors of his uniform. They enhanced David's personal coloring and made him look strikingly handsome.

In addition to the above reasons for the importance of our dress is its influence on our posture and movement. Our clothing affects the way we walk, run, bend, squat, kneel, or sit. It serves either to animate or to slow us down.

Society is aware of this principle and uses clothing to help enforce its rules of behavior. In practice, the dress codes of restaurants, schools, and other public and private institutions serve to control behavior as much as to control appearance.

I saw a practical example of this when I was serving as a trustee on a public school board. Because of certain discipline problems we were experiencing, we decided to experiment with a stricter, more formal dress code.

At first only the teachers participated and the discipline problems decreased slightly. We then imposed a mandatory dress code for students. Discipline problems decreased dramatically.

I discovered that this principle also worked at home. My mother once bought me a lovely, cherry red housecoat. I learned that the mornings I took time to brush my hair, touch my lips with a bit of color, and don my cheery cherry robe, my children's behavior and attitudes improved.

And when I paid closer attention to both the kind and condition of the clothing they wore, they voluntarily took a greater interest in their own appearance. I made sure the girls didn't get a boy's shirt that buttoned to the right. I took time to iron the pants that were borderline wrinkled. My efforts cost little in time or money, but the result was immediate improvement in my children's behavior.

All too often we allow ourselves to become so busy with our family that we don't think about being responsible for our appearance. We tell ourselves that we are working hard, even sacrificing for family members and children. We don't have time to pay much attention to the way we look, we say. In reality, such an attitude cheats us and all who are involved.

THE TEMPLE OF GOD

Most of us would feel concerned if the appearance of our church's property dropped below par. Unkempt pews, unwashed windows, streaked paint, torn carpets, and unmowed lawns would trouble us. Yet, as important as it is to care for church buildings, God's Word specifies that we are to take even better care of the appearance of our bodies.

Why? Because God tells us, "Know ye not that ye are the temple of God, and that the Spirit of God dwelleth in you? If any man defile the temple of God, him shall God destroy; for the temple of God is holy, which temple ye are" (1 Cor. 3:16, 17).

Whether or not we are aware of it, our appearance not only tells others how we view ourselves, but also indicates the quality of our relationship with God.

Our children are good witnesses of that.

Why? They see us as we really are, day in and day out. They see us at our best *and* at our worst. They see us early in the morning and late at night. They see us dressed up for church. They see us at other times as well.

Do they sometimes see you—the temple of the

Almighty God—with your body clad in a soiled robe or torn, unironed dress? Do you sometimes clothe your temple, or those of your children, in a manner unfitting its acclaimed Lord?

Jewish rabbis teach that you're supposed to wear your best clothes when you study the Torah, because they believe you come into the literal presence of Jehovah when you open his Word. Gentile Christians would do well to remember that we are never out of God's sight.

I'm not suggesting that we wear our best clothing all the time. But I am suggesting that we learn to make the most of what we have. My grandfather, for example, rarely possessed a new suit or new shoes. The ones he had were well worn. However, his suit was always neatly pressed, and his shirts were always bleached white from drying in the sun. And I never saw his shoes unpolished.

Every child is like a mirror: he reflects the influences around him and makes them his own. So if you do not project a belief that your body is the temple of God, you will never convince your child that his is.

A PERSONAL INVENTORY

Dressing well is not a frivolous or foolish occupation. No one should feel uncomfortable with how he has bedecked a temple of the living God. Listed below are a few questions that will help you determine your attitude toward dressing yourself.

1. Do you often feel you need to justify or apologize for the way you're dressed?

I once had a neighbor who did. No matter what time of day I knocked on her door, her invariable greeting was, "I look a fright. I'm sorry you have to see me looking like this." It was all too obvious that she wasn't sorry or she would have changed the situation.

2. Is your dress attractive to the people with whom you share common interests?

When people habitually wear jeans, they will feel intimidated or uncomfortable in the presence of those who are properly dressed. This can cause them to avoid moving into new social circles, and may even affect a chosen career.

Vera is an example. She was an attractive young law student who always wore jeans. So when she donned a dress for interviews, the unaccustomed garb caused her to move awkwardly. This was translated by her interviewers as uncertainty, resulting in the loss of excellent job opportunities.

In nature, careful grooming is basic to survival. In the north woods of Canada and Alaska, hungry timber wolves realize that unkempt caribou are easy prey. On the other hand, strong, healthy animals exhibit a well-kept, shiny coat. And unless the wolves are especially hungry, they will leave these stronger animals alone, preferring to tackle the ones who signal their tired or weak condition by their apparel. People send corresponding messages by their dress.

3. Is the daily act of dressing a pleasure?

When you wear something you don't especially like, it's impossible for you to feel at ease. One should aim to be neither clothes-conscious nor self-conscious, but rather, free from either concern. For when you feel comfortable with the way you are dressed, you can move with ease and speak with confidence. When you feel certain that you look good, you gain the freedom to concentrate on other people.

During your child's early years, you can inculcate him into the joy of good grooming. One way to do this is by placing coordinated clothes together in his drawer so he can choose a set for himself. A child that my daughters have baby-sat provides an example of what not to do. He is allowed to rummage through his drawers and put on anything he wishes.

This is grossly unfair to the child. He is not only *not* learning how to coordinate his clothing, but is also learning to think that anything is all right. As a consequence, Sammy consistently wears all kinds of odd combinations.

4. When you catch a glimpse of yourself in the mirror, do you like what you see?

Everyone has strengths, and everyone has weaknesses. But most of us are inclined to see our weaknesses and not notice our strengths. Pause for a few moments and make note of each of them in a list.

Remember that a weakness or a strength is only one if you believe it is. It must be dealt with accordingly, regardless of the facts. So try to think of ways to emphasize your strengths and minimize your weaknesses. You might also ask your children to make lists of their strengths and weaknesses. Discuss with them the ways they can stress their positive features.

5. Do you walk down the street feeling like an ambassador of God?

In the movie *Chariots of Fire*, Eric Liddell said, "When I run, I feel God's pleasure." We should learn to dress and conduct ourselves so we can feel God's pleasure in us because we look and act like extensions of him.

What most people expect to behold in your clothing is a harmonious whole. They appreciate not just nice separate articles of clothing, but a well-blended mix of pieces, undisturbed by clashes of color or style.

It seems incongruous to speak of my heavenly Father as the Creator of order and design when I, his creation, am decked out in a wild array of eye-jarring clothing. Since God does everything decently and in order, my manner of dressing myself, my husband, and my children should project the same quality. Everything about me—the words I speak, the clothing I wear, and the home I keep—should speak the same, consistent message.

Consistency is the word. It is useless, even presumptuous, for me to berate television's sex and violence, if my own body is not appropriately covered.

STRESS YOUR BEST

Each of us must come to terms with who we are and learn to accept ourselves. We can change many aspects of our circumstances, but it's not always easy to change others. Our body structure, our emotional makeup—these are usually permanent features.

But as important as it is to accept ourselves, such acceptance doesn't have to mean resignation to "reality." Many of the personal attributes that may seem to be flaws can easily be disguised or deemphasized.

Thelma is a case in point. She didn't like the shape of her arms. For several years this upset her to the point that she refused to appear in public without wearing a coat or large bulky sweater.

Then one day a friend of hers said, "Thelma, that's ridiculous. You have a very pretty face. Emphasize your face and deemphasize your arms."

"I don't know how," Thelma wailed.

"Let me show you."

A few days later, Thelma was a transformed person. Instead of the short, severe blouses she frequently wore, she appeared in a long-sleeved, tastefully selected cotton blouse. The high, ruffled neckline, accentuated with pretty jewelry just below her chin, drew attention to her lovely face. The ruffled cuffs drew attention to her well-shaped hands.

"I feel like a different person," Thelma told her friend.

"You *are* different, because now you can view yourself differently."

Thelma had learned to direct the observer's eye to her strengths through the use of skillfully applied makeup and carefully selected clothing. She learned the principle that just as every good photograph or painting has a focal point, so should every ensemble you create.

Any of us can choose which of our qualities we desire to feature. It only makes sense to stress the best. All of us possess certain characteristics we consider either good or not-so-good. So it's up to you to emphasize your good points and deemphasize your not-so-good areas.

Properly used, clothing becomes an extension of the body. So if a person doesn't like his physical image, he most likely has trouble with his clothing image as well. If anyone is convinced that his body is unattractive, then it is. *Because reality for one's self is what he believes.*

I personally know a number of slender, attractive young women who are so convinced that they are either fat or ugly that they have become unapproachable introverts. More than one such girl has so deprived herself of food in order to lose weight that she has harmed both her physical and mental health.

One must examine himself in the light of God's Word. If God says I am loved, then I am. And if God says I am beautiful, then I am. It's up to me to make the best use of what I perceive with my physical eyes so that I will conform to the image of the loveliness that God attributes to me.

My husband, Bob, is nearly six feet tall. He has very long legs and a disproportionately short torso. For most of his adult life, he was embarrassed by the length of his legs. Not knowing what to do about his problem, he dressed himself in baggy pants, held up with a wide leather belt and a huge belt buckle. And he frequently wore jackets that were much too long. All of these things even further emphasized his short torso.

But when I convinced him that his long legs were

an *asset* to his appearance if he dressed properly, he began to remedy the situation. One of the ways he did this was by wearing well-fitted slacks with either a narrow belt or no belt at all. The result is a long and pleasing lean look.

DRESSING YOUR CHILD

The manner in which you choose to dress usually accents a certain aspect of your physique or your personality. Whatever aspect you habitually display will become stronger and more predominant in your life. This is true for anyone, but especially for a child. The traits that parents emphasize will become the traits the child most strongly projects.

As a small child, Raymond was gentle and soft-spoken. But Raymond's daddy loved Western movies and read only Western magazines. As a result, he always dressed his small son in cowboy clothes with pistols at his hips. Father and son addressed each other as "pardner" and used Western slang. Raymond's family and friends thought this was cute.

By the time Raymond started to school, it was evident that all of this playacting had affected the little boy. His behavior now depicted that of a rough, tough cowboy. He was no longer soft-spoken.

Raymond actually became the character he played. His continual exposure to Western clothing, Western movies, and rough speech did its work. The gentle little boy was transformed into a swaggering, over-bearing bully—an exact replica of the heroes he had learned to admire.

Like Raymond's parents, your early choices about your child's appearance will have a profound effect upon the way his personality develops.

This truth became clear to us in a new way as we hosted and conducted Bible studies in our home.

Many of the young women among us eagerly desired to become wives and homemakers. But those who had always worn jeans and coveralls, to the virtual exclusion of gowns and dresses, had great difficulty feeling comfortable with their identity as women.

Jessie, in particular, evinced this problem. Though she was raised in better than average circumstances, both of her parents were professionals and paid little attention to their young daughter. As a result, Jessie wasn't really "raised," she just grew up—like a weed. Since no one cared about the way she dressed, Jessie took the way of least resistance. She dressed like the boys she played with.

"I *never* wore dresses," she told us. "None of my close friends wore dresses. We even made fun of the girls who wore them."

And now, when Jessie strongly desires to project a more feminine image, she struggles with the patterns established during her early years. "I just don't feel comfortable in a dress," she says.

It's easy to see that this is true. Even though she is preparing for a career that will require appropriately feminine professional attire, Jessie looks very ill at ease in a dress. As it always does, this dilemma has caused Jessie great difficulty with her self-image.

You can count on this inviolable truth: Young people respond to life's situations in exactly the same manner in which they have been prepared. In Jessie's case, now that she is actually becoming what she is to be, her emotional growth corresponds with the care invested in the "soil" of her femininity.

My husband and I recently dealt with a young woman who possessed strong homosexual tendencies. One of Rosemarie's major difficulties was her lack of identification with her mother or anything feminine in nature. As a result, Rosemarie consistently dressed herself in men's pants and hats. Rosemarie's clothing image fed her inner image until the girl related her identity with what she continually saw in her mirror.

Christian women should be careful not to dress in fabrics or styles that cause them to look like men; nor should they allow their daughters to grow up feeling more comfortable looking like boys than girls. God speaks strongly to this principle: "The woman shall not wear that which pertaineth unto a man, neither shall a man put on a woman's garment: for all that do so are abomination unto the Lord thy God" (Deut. 22:5). To violate God's laws in this matter will bring confusion and suffering to our children.

DISCOVER YOUR COLORS

Recently my daughter Trish took advanced college classes at UCLA in fashion and color design. Trish's professor used the seasons of the year to describe the color categories into which all persons fit, regardless of their ethnic origin. Trish learned that, just as God has given special, harmonious colors to each of the seasons, he also has provided each of our bodies with a distinct coloring, one that is best complemented by one of the seasonal palettes.

To illustrate:

The person complemented by the *winter* palette is stunning in clear, vivid primary and cool colors; like an eye-catching black tree laced with glittering white snowflakes.

The person complemented by the *spring* palette comes alive in delicate colors with warm yellow under-tones; like the fresh green leaves of the first tulips that bloom each spring.

The person complemented by the *summer* palette is pleasing in the soft colors of the sea and sky, with their cool blue undertones; like the ravishing colors of June's flower garden.

The person complemented by the *autumn* palette is radiant in warm, rich colors with golden undertones; like the splashes of brown, red-orange, and forest green in an October woods.

No one needs to look pale and lifeless as long as he wears a shade that brings out the glow of his natural coloring. Each of us has a unique skin tone. And the discovery of the colors that best complement this tone brings out our special beauty.

The genes that determine your skin tone, hair, and eye color also determine which colors look best on you. When you carefully study your personal coloring, you will find that your skin, hair, and eyes possess either blue or golden tones. *It is those blue or golden tones—not your skin color*—that determine your color palette. For example, persons with deep black skin and those with very fair white skin may all be of the winter palette.

Remember that your inherited skin tone does not change; it simply deepens with a tan and fades with age. The same color palette will always look the best on you.

In her UCLA classes, Trish also learned the technique of draping to determine a person's palette season. This is done by placing swatches of the various seasonal colors around the shoulders of the person being tested for his or her palette season. Draping should be done in as much natural light as possible. Women should remove makeup before the draping, since any trace of color would affect the palette determination.

As swatches of colored cloth are placed on the subject one at a time, a skilled eye can note how the right colors enhance the person's face, while the wrong shades detract from it.

Even the untrained eye can quickly tell the difference between "right" and "wrong" colors. The right colors will call attention to the person's face, causing onlookers to notice how well he or she looks. On the other hand, the wrong colors will shout, "Look at me!" and call attention to the garment instead of the subject.

As Trish and I became more and more interested in the enhancing effects of the right colors, we began draping all the young people who came to Bible study—the young men as well as the young ladies. We immediately noted that a pleasing and rather startling transformation began taking place among all the young people, irregardless of sex, age, education, or economics.

As the young people began wearing their own special colors, they soon were receiving compliments such as, "How lovely you look!" (to the ladies) and, "You look great in that outfit!" (to the men). All of this naturally made them feel better about themselves, and so the upward spiral began.

They learned: Change your outward appearance for the better, and people will respond differently toward you. . . .

Which means: Your self-esteem is increased, leading to positive changes in your behavior. . . .

And then: People respond even more favorably toward you.

The result: Your self-esteem is even further enhanced, enabling you to move in directions not possible before.

Peter is an exciting example of these principles. He was partially crippled and had struggled with a weak, inadequate self-concept all his life. He was quite introverted and tended to take a back seat in about every area of his life.

After we draped Peter, he got excited about the possibilities of enhancing his looks. We helped him buy some new clothes in his color palette. The transforming process began immediately.

Within a couple of weeks, Peter asked to read the

Scripture at Bible study, then a few weeks later he requested permission to teach a Bible study session. His new confidence was showing and he did an excellent job.

By the end of the year, he was in training to become a lay minister in his church. He was asked to preach in his church and received many compliments from his pastor and friends.

Peter literally became what his mirror showed him. The power of God's Holy Spirit, working on the inside of Peter, completed the transformation.

God tells us to love and help one another. In so doing, we strengthen each other and the whole body of Christ. Nowhere have we seen the impact of our help more than in our color testing and draping.

The practice of color draping has caught on in our community and social circle. Trish and I frequently receive calls requesting us to help someone with their colors and wardrobe. A few weeks ago, we were asked to go to a school for the handicapped by a handicapped person who had so profited from a color draping at our house that he wanted to share his gains in the name of Jesus.

To see the delighted response of people as they come alive before our very eyes is indescribable! We see them catch a vision of how to improve their looks, and, in the process, their own feelings about themselves. The positive results we witness are far out of proportion to the effort we expend.

Common to all people is the strong desire to grow and to learn, to take better control of their own lives and destinies. We can prepare them to do this by helping them to feel better about themselves.

CHOOSING YOUR CHILD'S COLORS
Parents should never take lightly their children's desire to make themselves as attractive as possible. Children

who feel good about themselves will inevitably do better in school than those who don't.

So it will benefit you and your entire family when you use the seasonal palettes to select colors in which you—and they—glow with vitality. Remember, some faces come alive when they are surrounded by clear, bright colors; other faces require softer colors.

I look my best in the winter palette, as does my mother. Not understanding as much about colors when my first daughter, Trish, was born, I dressed her in my preferred colors from the winter palette. Then when Alíce came along, she inherited her sister's clothes.

As a child Alíce looked prettier than her older sister, and I didn't understand why at the time. But the primary colors I dressed the girls in caused Alíce to glow, while they completely washed out Trish's face.

Interestingly enough, when I allowed her to do so, Trish would often naturally choose the best colors for her looks.

At this point, it would be helpful to go back to chapter 6 and reread the section on the psychological and physiological effects of color. In everyone's color palette there are colors that excite and calm, stimulate and relax. I realize that red was physiologically a helpful color for Alíce. But the same color exerted a definite negative effect upon Trish by increasing her already high natural activity level. So take time to understand your use of color.

Now that I know more about color, I notice that many people around me are making the same mistake I made when my children were small. That is, they are dressing their children and spouses in their own special colors, rather than the ones that best enhance each individual.

Numerous books on the market (mostly for women) on the subject of color go into much greater detail than is appropriate for this book. However, there is a delightful coloring book on the market that's geared specifically for helping *your child* learn to choose his or her own personal colors and clothes. To receive details, send a self-addressed, postpaid envelope to: *Color Your Colors*, P.O. Box 854, Pacific Palisades, CA 90272.

WHAT DOES YOUR FACE SAY?

It is good for everyone to systematically check his face in a mirror, not only for the impact of the color of his clothes, but also for the effect of his expressions. Since the face is the primary focus of communication, it behooves each of us to know what our friends see when they look at us.

Children, too, should do this. Though a child is not responsible for the total appearance of his face at age two, he definitely is by the time he reaches adulthood. What better time to begin to train him than when he is small.

In front of a mirror you learn what your smile looks like. Your smile, or lack of it, is one of the first aspects of your public appearance that others respond to.

The frequency of a two-year-old's smile depends on what he sees in his environment. The frequency—and quality—of a forty-two-year-old's smile depends on what he sees *within himself.* And every adult is responsible for himself. Contrary to some opinions, facial muscles, like other muscles, are trainable. You *can* teach yourself to smile!

Such training begins with the thoughts one is thinking. Pleasant thoughts prompt pleasant expressions. The reverse is also true. Like your smiles, the thoughts behind them must also be practiced.

God tells us how to practice good thoughts. "Fix your thoughts on what is true and good and right. Think about things that are pure and lovely, and dwell on the fine, good things in others. Think about all you can praise God for and be glad about" (Phil. 4:8, TLB).

The more you practice pleasant thoughts and their expression, the more spontaneous they become. In chapter 7 of *The Idea Book for Mothers,* I give an exercise that you and your child can do together to help develop your smiling muscles. For even as you train your child to hold a pencil and tie a shoe with his hands, you can teach him to express a happy look with his face.

But the most effective help you can provide your child is to keep before him a pleasant demeanor, because he will model what he sees. And the practice will do you both good, because when a smile starts on the face, it usually spreads to the spirit.

THE ROBE OF CONFIDENCE

When I was a student in the eighth grade, two new girls, Rachel and Stella, joined my gym class in the same week. The picture of that event is indelibly engraved on my memory.

Stella had wavy light brown hair and was slightly overweight. She wore a new pair of plaid shorts and a purple sweatshirt. My gym instructor made a passing reference to Stella as being new to our community and our class.

That was Stella's introduction.

Rachel's introduction was totally different.

She was trim and pretty. Her long, black hair was saucily tied back with a bright red ribbon. She was dressed in white shirt, shorts, and tennis shoes, all appearing to be well-worn, washed, and bleached many times.

She came to class three days after Stella. Our instructor said, "Rachel, come up front. I want the girls to meet you."

Then she was lavishly introduced. "We're glad to have such an attractive young lady in our gym class. . . ."

I know that the way these two girls were welcomed to our class had a distinct bearing on the way they adjusted to the new environment. Rachel knew everybody's name within a few days, while it took Stella most of the semester to make friends.

As I have pondered this incident, my mind has been drawn to numerous case studies conducted on school children. Many of these studies indicate that most teachers favor attractive and well-dressed children. Yet without a doubt, Stella was physically the more attractive of the two girls. Her clothes were newer and obviously more expensive. Then why did Rachel get "top billing" while Stella was barely recognized?

Actually, the term *attractive* is sometimes misleading. It does not necessarily refer to symmetry of face or form, the cost of clothing, the color or amount of hair. Rather, it implies a contagious confidence that springs from the joy of just being who we are.

Such confidence imparts an inner glow, an inner beauty that is not limited to physical characteristics.

Contrary to popular thought, attractiveness is not necessarily beyond the reach of anyone—if only we'd learn to approach the subject of beauty from the perspective of the Word of God.

For the most part, others don't fix a disdainful eye on our pointed chin, our extra broad shoulders, or even our crooked nose. They look at the whole person in front of them. And what they see is something you can determine more than you might think.

They see the way you carry yourself. "Thou, O Lord, art . . . my glory, and the lifter up of mine head" (Ps. 3:3). When you know who you are in God's sight, you will carry yourself with pride and confidence.

They see how straight and firm you stand. "Stand

fast . . . in the liberty wherewith Christ hath made us free" (Gal. 5:1). When your life is planted upon Jesus the Rock, your upright posture will reflect your stability.

They see how gracefully you move. "For in him we live, and move, and have our being" (Acts 17:28). Minor details of physiognomy will be unimportant when people see you moving in the grace and power of God.

They see how your clothes fit you. "The Spirit of the Lord clothed Gideon with Himself" (Judges 6:34, AMP). And what better fit could one have than one tailored by God himself?

They see how alive your face is. "And all of us, with unveiled face, because we continued to behold in the Word of God as in a mirror the glory of the Lord, are constantly being transfigured into His very own image" (2 Cor. 3:18, AMP). It was said of Stephen, the first martyr, that his face shone as an angel's (Acts 6:15). When your face shines with the inner glory of God, others will notice hardly anything else about you.

When people see the above Scriptures exemplified in you, you need have little concern about minor physical imperfections. They will respond to God's likeness in you. Because, you see, most people respond not to the beauty that's inherited, but to the kind that grows.

CHANGE TAKES TIME

But as in anything else, changes—including those described above—cannot be achieved overnight. They develop slowly as you consistently work at them.

Like all girls, I wanted so very much to look pretty when I was young. But as I studied myself in the mirror, all I saw was a bumpy-looking face, and I decided that I wasn't pretty at all. It took months and years of learning how to eat properly (see chapter 8) and take care of my skin before I could look into the mirror and feel good about myself.

It even took time for me to learn to properly emphasize my naturally wavy hair, my deep-set eyes, and my petite figure. But when I learned how to appreciate what I was and emphasize my strengths, life took on new meaning for me.

Ellie is another case in point. Her face was physically beautiful. But she tended to be chronically overweight. It took years of training herself to eat and exercise properly before she felt good about her total appearance.

Sandy's difficult birth affected her ability to properly control the movements of her limbs. It took persistence and years of ballet dancing as an adult before she could walk and move gracefully.

All of these corrective changes took years of persistent new seed-planting before a successful harvest was reaped.

About 180 B.C. the son of Sirach wrote in the Book of Ecclesiasticus, "A man shall be known by his appearance." This is still true today.

By emphasizing your own positive attributes, you will inspire confidence in yourself. You can learn to make people happy just to be in your presence. You can create in them a desire to know the God you take such delight in representing.

And in doing all of this, you will properly prepare the soil of your child's image so that it accurately reflects the beauty of our God's creation.

8: HOW TO REAP HEALTH

The three of us—Dr. Allan, Pastor Corey, and I—just stood there, gazing down at her. After a long while the woman in the hospital bed opened her eyes. I flinched involuntarily when I saw the pain mirrored in her dark black eyes, pain that almost reached out and touched us.

Her deep-set eyes moved from one to the other of us. She took a deep breath and struggled to speak. We leaned over to hear her scarcely whispered words.

"There's no need for any more surgery, Dr. Allan . . . no need to pray for my healing, Pastor Corey . . . no need to talk any more, Pat. . . ."

She paused again and I took her cold hand in my

two warm ones. She closed her eyes for a long moment and I thought she was asleep. Then she drew a long, shuddering breath and opened her eyes again. "I didn't want God to let me die," she whispered again, "but finally I understand why . . . 'My belly was my God and now destruction is my end.' "

The doctor and pastor looked at each other. Nobody spoke.

"Tell them, Pat," Linnette whispered, weaker than before. "Tell them . . . tell everyone. . . . It's the cumulative effect. . . ."

The room was filled with the quiet of death, but in my ears, Linnette's soft voice was shouting, "Tell everyone, tell everyone, everyone. . . ."

It's in response to Linnette's dying plea that I write this chapter.

THE CUMULATIVE EFFECT

Joel is a young pastor who unquestionably loves the Lord. He was raised in the church and has lived an upright life. He is a kind husband and father to his wife and three children. The church he pastors is growing under his leadership, and he is well accepted in the community.

There's only one problem: Joel is sick much of the time.

"I don't understand it," he says. "I believe God wants his children to prosper and be healthy. He told us that many times in his Word. But it's difficult to preach that message when my own body isn't well."

As he spoke, Joel munched on a doughnut. "The doctor admits he's baffled," the young pastor said, sipping his coffee. "He has taken X rays and given me all kinds of tests, but he doesn't find anything wrong. He gives me antibiotics, and I seem to do better for a while. Then I'm right back where I was before. It's discouraging."

Joel's experience is not unusual. Doctors find their waiting rooms filled with people who complain of vague aches and pains. They say, "I'm just not feeling up to par," or "I'm tired all the time," or "I don't rest well."

I can personally identify with these complaints. When I was raising my five children, there were often times when I hardly had enough energy to get out of bed or to go about the business of living.

It wasn't until all of my children were grown, and I was working as public relations director for a Christian university, that I fully realized that something was wrong. The position was very demanding. My office was often full of people; others waited outside. My telephone was usually ringing.

Besides, there were letters to write, luncheon engagements to fill, a monthly PR magazine to produce, special projects to handle—the list was endless.

By midmorning I was nearly always exhausted. By midafternoon I could scarcely drag myself around. When I finally made it home in the evening, I was so weary that I could barely make it to bed. I was plagued with colitis and constant, pounding headaches. To make matters even worse, there were entire days when I found myself on the verge of tears.

My husband expressed concern.

I was defensive. "I'm all right," I said. "I'm just working too hard."

"I know that," he agreed, "but I believe it would help if you would begin your day by eating breakfast."

"I don't have time. I'll pick up a cup of coffee and a doughnut in the cafeteria."

He shook his head. "That's not food," he said. "That's junk. And it's doing you more harm than good."

"All right, then," I said, "I'll drink a glass of milk with my doughnut."

In the back of my mind, I realized he was right. But I had a job to do. I was a busy executive. My work demanded a lot from me. All of this was true, but it was *not* the reason for my problems.

It was harvesttime and my problem was *the kind of harvest I was reaping.* And because this harvest was the result of cumulative reaping, nothing I did seemed to change anything. My colitis persisted, and my headaches grew worse.

The cumulation might have continued if my husband hadn't started writing a book entitled *Sugar Merchants.* He researched the subject for many months before he began writing. While he was doing this research, we became aware of the importance of the foods we were eating—or *not eating,* as was the case much of the time.

We soon came face to face with the fact that God's natural laws also apply to our diet. Those who live according to them reap their benefits; likewise, those who break them suffer for their violations.

A simple example: Air is for breathing, while water is for drinking. If we attempt to violate these laws by breathing water, we'll drown.

The law of gravity is another example. By holding us to the earth's surface, gravity prevents us from being flung off into outer space. However, if we misuse this natural law by stepping off a high building, we will suffer the consequences.

God has provided proper food for us to eat (Gen. 1:29). As long as a person feeds his body as God intended, he reaps a harvest of health. But when he stops feeding his body properly, he will reap a different kind of harvest.

Such a harvest may begin with the appearance of small symptoms—not feeling up to par, for example.

But one must not deceive himself. If the wrong kind of sowing persists, the inevitable cumulative effect will be ill health, suffering, and an untimely death.

Fact: The United States is one of the most affluent nations on earth, with one of the highest standards of living.

Fact: In spite of our affluence, Americans rank first in many illnesses—cancer, heart disease, hypertension, diabetes, and mental illness.

All of these illnesses, say a growing number of nutritionists, are directly related to the foods we eat. According to a July 10, 1984, article in *USA Today*, the American Cancer Society, National Cancer Institute, and National Academy of Sciences recommend eating "high fiber foods daily . . . whole-grain foods and fresh vegetables and fruit." These foods, they say, "will cut the risk of certain kinds of cancer."

In the same article, John Weisburger of the American Health Foundation says, "Seventy-five percent of colon cancer and 50 percent of breast cancer could be prevented by reducing fats and increasing fiber in the diet."

In his book *Dr. Atkins' Superenergy Diet* (Bantam, 1978), Robert C. Atkins makes a startling statement. "The American population is a diseased population," he says. "Most American people are eating a totally unhealthy diet and have been eating so poorly all their lives that we accept poor health as the norm, unaware of how well we can really function."

Our bodies literally *become* what we put into them. In other words, if you put *live* food, such as fresh fruit and vegetables, nuts, grains, and seeds into your body, you will lengthen your life. (Incidentally, *all* chewable seeds, including apple seeds, grape seeds, and orange seeds are rich in nutritious fiber and the cancer-fighting B-17.)

If you put *dead* food—processed foods, the so-called

junk foods, foods filled with preservatives—into your body, you will diminish the quality of your life and hasten your death. So ask yourself the question, "What did I eat today that would grow if I planted it in the ground?"

During his high school years, my son Keith worked for a mortician. One day Mr. Schipper explained to Keith that Americans require less embalming than some years ago.

Keith asked, "Why is that?"

"Because most of the food they eat is so filled with preservatives that, by the time they die, their bodies are already partially embalmed."

MALNUTRITION

As a consequence of not eating natural, balanced diets, millions of people also suffer from malnutrition. "Mal" simply means bad. Being malnourished means you lack the proper kinds and amounts of minerals and vitamins.

Due to malnutrition, many people feel poorly most of the time. They lack vim, vigor, and the get-up-and-get-going power to carry out the duties of life. They drag themselves through the day—as I did—often feeling exhausted.

This exhaustion is the reason many people turn to stimulants such as tea, coffee, chocolate, cola drinks (all of which are rich in caffeine), tobacco, alcohol, and even other drugs to pep them up for a while. But after the effects of these stimulants wear off, they feel terrible.

Included among the millions of malnourished people are many Christians. Because of their poor eating habits, these believers are unable to live the more abundant life that Jesus promised as our heritage.

Is abundant life affected by the food I eat?

Yes. Without proper nutrition, your body lacks the necessary building materials to properly replace worn tissues and sustain life. In fact, if your family is existing on junk foods or an inadequate diet, you are literally killing yourself and your children.

If you eat the wrong kinds of food, you might get by with it for today, or this year, or maybe even next year. But the cumulative effect of God's Genesis Principle is inviolable. You will reap what you sow from poor eating habits.

In his book *Everything You Always Wanted to Know About Nutrition,* David Reuben says, "It is incomprehensible to me that intelligent people have not made the obvious . . . connection between the chemicalized, denutrified, contaminated, deeply embalmed garbage we incorrectly refer to as a 'modern diet' and the directly resulting diseases that *each year kill more than twice as many Americans as perished in all the many wars the United States has ever fought.*

"People of America," Reuben warns, "the greatest threat to the survival of you and your children is not some terrible nuclear weapon. *It is what you are going to eat from your dinner plates tonight."* (Emphasis added.)

The effects of malnutrition span the gamut of our health problems. Some doctors express alarm over the rising incidence of infertility among both men and women. One doctor, in an interview on a national TV show, blamed this increased infertility upon "the large amounts of preservatives and chemicals—including medicines and other drugs—being introduced into our bodies."

Recently a young woman in my son's Bible study group asked him to pray that the Lord would heal her terrible skin problem. It seems that her face had been covered with ugly, running sores for months. Marilyn had been unsuccessfully treated with shots and medications for many weeks.

When she asked David to pray for God to heal her, he answered, "Of course I'll pray for you. But you should also talk to my father. He'll explain God's natural healing laws to you."

So the girl called Bob. He immediately asked about her diet. Bob told her, "If you'll eliminate certain foods from your diet and eat the ones I tell you, I believe your skin will clear up in a few weeks."

"I'll do exactly what you tell me," she said.

Three weeks later Marilyn came to Bible study. Her face had cleared up beautifully, leaving her with smooth skin. No one would have suspected that just days before she had feared to appear in public because of her blemished complexion.

"It's a miracle of healing," the girl told us.

"Yes," my husband said, "a *natural-law* miracle that God set in motion at the time of creation. You have merely allowed that natural law the freedom to operate by feeding your body living food."

FOOD ADVERTISEMENTS

I have talked to many people who honestly would like to improve their diets, but they say, "There is so much confusing advertising about nutrition that I don't know who or what to believe."

Radio, TV, magazines, newspapers, and even billboards shout conflicting messages hundreds of times a day: "Buy this bread," "Drink this soft drink—it's the best!" "This lunch meat is the most nutritious." The list could go on.

Just last night as I was watching TV, I saw a highly creative advertisement for a nationally known brand of bread. "Good nutrition doesn't have to be whole wheat," the actor on the commercial said. "Maybe it doesn't have as many nutrients and fibers as whole wheat bread. But *our bread* has important minerals such as calcium, niacin, and iron."

The ad was so cleverly put together that, even though the bread company made no *legally* incorrect statements, the effect was deliberately misleading. For what the ad did not say was that the flour they used to make their white bread had been devitalized while being milled.

Refined, bleached white flour has had forty-four of its valuable nutrients removed in whole or in part, leaving a product that even some bugs will not eat. Then, as an advertising gimmick, the processors put back into the devitalized flour about one-sixth of a penny's worth of cheap, synthetic vitamins consisting of thiamin, riboflavin, and niacin, and a tiny bit of iron, often in the form of iron filings. They label their product *enriched!*

Admittedly, all of this advertising is very confusing to the average person. That's the idea. If the consumer can't understand it, the marketers believe he'll buy it without asking any questions.

Many consumers, perhaps including yourself, ask, "But don't advertisers have to tell the truth about their products?" The answer is a resounding no! In some cases they are required to list the ingredients on their products, but in many cases they are not.

If you can't trust the advertisers, who can you trust?

The answer is yourself.

Learn the basics of nutrition. Take time to find out all you can about the food you eat so that you and your family can live in health.

I personally want to encourage you to begin this adventure in good nutrition. And *it is* an adventure. It's a new way of living that's done wonders for me and for my family. As a direct result of good nutrition, I don't remember the last time when I had a cold or a headache.

It's wonderful to live in good health! With all my heart, I thank God for the knowledge of how to eat right.

Do you remember the story in Matthew 9:36–38, where Jesus was moved with compassion because the people were like sheep without a shepherd? He said, "Pray ye therefore the Lord of the harvest, that he will send forth labourers into his harvest" (Matt. 9:38).

Well, I prayed for laborers to show us the way to a more abundant, healthy life. God sent them to us, and he will do the same for you. Ask him to help you find someone you can trust to lead you along the pathway to health.

To help you get started, I will give you some practical ways to implement the basics of nutrition.

CHANGE YOUR DIET SLOWLY

The first thing I want to impress upon you is this: *Don't try to change all of your eating habits at once!* It can't be done. You will only discourage yourself with the complexities of the task. But do begin to learn which foods are harmful for you, and start avoiding them one at a time, in small increments.

As you select and prepare nutritious foods for yourself and your family, you will one day—a week or a month later—wake up feeling like you haven't felt in years. You will be overwhelmed with a sense of well-being. And you will say, as I've heard many say, "I had forgotten what it was like to feel so good."

Before you get to that point, you may have some discouraging days. You may feel like all your favorite foods have disappeared. You may begin to wonder if food can taste good and be healthy at the same time.

Let me reassure you, personal food tastes are cultivated. Likes and dislikes are learned. That's the reason Mexican children enjoy hot peppers, Japanese children like raw fish, and African children like their "tasty" fried grasshoppers.

That's also the reason why the average American teenager thinks he cannot live without his hamburger, french fries, and cola. In each case, the tastes have been learned. And in each case, these tastes can be changed.

When my husband and I began our search for good nutrition, one of the first foods I realized I must give up was chocolate. I craved chocolate and ate some nearly every day. It was difficult for me to give it up. But I was determined to begin properly feeding myself and my family.

It took time—months and months of eating right— before I suddenly realized one day that I no longer craved chocolate. In fact, it seemed to be rather sickeningly sweet. That day I made the exciting discovery that my tastes really could change!

Like my yen for chocolate, all of your food likes and dislikes have been learned. Often you acquired your tastes when you were so young that you don't remember when you first began liking certain foods. So, just as you learned to eat some foods, you can learn to eat others—those that are as good or even better for you than what you have been accustomed to eating.

Actually, it's a matter of will. If you decide to eat what is nutritionally good for your body, instead of allowing your tastes to dictate your diet, you have already won half the battle.

In teaching your children how to eat new foods, begin on a positive note. Don't nag them by saying, "Don't eat that because it's bad for you."

Instead, tell them, "Your body is the temple of the living God. Your body is marvelous—too marvelous to be polluted with stuff like that." This positive approach emphasizes the privilege of learning to care for God's wonderful creation. It creates an opportunity, rather than a deprivation.

UNDERSTAND FOOD ADDITIVES

Learn to read and understand labels. Again, this takes time. Don't be panicked into trying to handle this responsibility all at once. But as you begin reading the labels on packaged or processed foods, you will soon discover a number of items to avoid. Just because you have always eaten a certain product does not mean it is good for you.

For example, a loaf of white bread contains a lengthy list of additives and chemicals to retard spoilage and keep the bread from rotting on the shelves. (When you shop for food, a helpful saying to keep in mind is, "Don't eat food if it won't rot. But do eat food before it rots.")

There are many additives in our foods today, including emulsifiers, stabilizers, and calcium sulphate (nothing more than plaster of paris, which holds the piece of junk together). In some cases, brown bread labeled "whole wheat" is produced by simply adding caramel coloring to the white paste.

What the labels fail to tell you is that many of these additives can hurt the consumer. For instance, see if you can buy a package of processed meat that does not have sodium nitrite or sodium nitrate in it. Both of these products are *proven carcinogens,* yet they have not been banned from our foods. Meanwhile, the debates go on and on about the amount of carcinogens a body can handle before cancer develops.

I encourage you to begin checking the meanings of the words on labels. The bibliography at the end of the chapter will guide you to books that will help you begin this adventure.

You need to develop this skill yourself, because you

can't totally trust all so-called health food stores. Bob visited one yesterday to purchase a product he knew he could trust. The young man at the cash register recommended another product of a similar nature. He was so excited about it that he took Bob to the shelf and handed him the item.

Being familiar with the product, Bob asked him, "Does it have any detrimental additives?"

Surprised at Bob's question, the young man said, "Well, let's check the list of ingredients." Suddenly a shocked expression came to his face.

"The first one on the list is harmful!" he said. "I didn't know it, because I've never looked at the label before."

AVOID HARMFUL FOODS

Listed and explained below are several foods common to most American diets: refined sugar, refined flour, and caffeine beverages. They should all be avoided.

Refined Sugar. In 1972 an international scientific convention in West Germany recommended that people stop eating sugar. Their stated reason, reports Robert C. Atkins, was "that sugar is a killer, not only for you, but for your family" *(Everything You Always Wanted to Know About Nutrition).* Attending the convention were world-recognized experts on diabetes, obesity, metabolism, and arteriosclerosis (hardening of the arteries).

The sugar they referred to is refined sugar, found in practically every home in the country. Contrary to what the sugar industry would have us believe, refined sugar is *not* a natural food. In fact, it's not a food at all. It is a pure chemical extracted from plant sources, purer in fact than cocaine, which it resembles in many ways.

Refined sugar has no vitamins, no useful minerals,

no enzymes, no trace elements, no fiber, no protein, no fat, and *no benefit whatsoever in the human diet.*

The sugar industry is big business, one of the biggest food businesses in the world. Annual sugar sales in the United States alone add up to nearly *ten billion dollars.* This industry has sold the public a bill of goods that touts sugar as being an excellent source of energy. It is a source of energy, but not the kind of energy you want.

"The truth is," says Reuben, "that sugar will only make you fat. And even worse, if you're tired and lacking in pep, a good slug of refined sugar will only give you a very brief 'high.' Then you will soon be even more lethargic than before, and ravenously hungry."

But what about brown sugar? Or raw sugar? The brown sugar and raw sugar you see at the grocery store are simply refined sugars colored with molasses or food coloring. They are just as empty of food value and just as destructive as the white variety.

Don't be deceived into using disguised versions of sugar. The industry will try to fool you with such names as dextrose, fructose, glucose, sorbitol, corn syrup, and other synonyms. All of these are forms of sugar that should be avoided.

Fructose is marketed with the claim that it's a natural replacement for refined sugar. This is misleading, however, since most of the fructose sold commercially is produced from corn syrup, a form of refined sugar.

What about honey, pure maple syrup, date sugar (made from finely ground dried dates), and unsulphured molasses? These are examples of unrefined sugar, which is different than refined sugar.

All refined sugars consist of empty calories, which bring no food value to your body. Even worse, they *deplete* your body of certain minerals and vitamins that are vital for good nutrition.

Unrefined sugars, however, possess several vitamins

and trace minerals. This means that in the metabolism
of such sugars, the body is not robbed as it is with
refined sugars.

Personally, though I use unrefined sugars in my
cooking and baking, I use them sparingly. In and of
themselves they are not harmful, but they still are
sugar, and their overuse will cause problems. "Hast
thou found honey?" asks the writer of the Proverbs.
"Eat so much as is sufficient for thee. . . ." Then he
adds this warning, "It is not good to eat much honey"
(Prov. 25:16, 27).

This statement proves true in daily life. Many studies
have explored the possible connection between sugar
addiction—yes, sugar addiction—and crime. One of
these studies, directed by Alexander G. Schauss for
the state of California, showed that "more crimes were
committed under the influence of sugar than even
under the effect of alcohol or hard drugs. The large
amounts of sugar came in the form of candy bars,
doughnuts, pastries, ice cream, Jell-O, boxed cereals,
coffee, Koolaid, and soda pop."

One such crime was the "Twinkie murder" of Mayor
Musconie of San Francisco. The much-publicized
crime received this name because the murderer, Dan
White, was found by psychologists to have been hyped-
up by Twinkies and other heavily sugared products
when he committed the crime.

Refined Flour. Though I briefly touched on this subject
when I discussed the advertisement of white bread, I
would like to insert an additional word about refined
flour, from which most bakery products are made.

A grain of wheat consists of bran, wheat germ, and
endosperm. (See the illustration in this chapter.) The
bran and wheat germ are the fiber and nutrition of
the wheat. The endosperm by itself is basically worthless bulk.

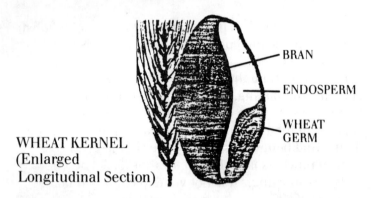

WHEAT KERNEL
(Enlarged
Longitudinal Section)

It's in the milling process that whole wheat kernels become something less than whole grain flour, which, when baked, produces something less than *whole* wheat bread. Excessive milling removes the bran and wheat germ, leaving only the next to worthless endosperm. And it is from this endosperm, known as refined white flour, that most bread is made. Even some so-called whole wheat bread is *not* whole grain bread, but milled white flour that is dyed with food coloring.

In Isaiah 28, God speaks against the destructive milling process. "Grain for bread is crushed, indeed, he does not continue to thresh it forever. Because the wheel of his cart and his horses eventually damage it, He does not thresh it longer. This also comes from the Lord of hosts, who has made His counsel wonderful and His wisdom great" (Isa. 28:28, 29, NASB).

As the above Scripture infers, whole grain flour is made by simply grinding the whole kernels into coarse flour from which *nothing is extracted.*

The bran in whole grain flour is crucial to good health. There is little doubt that the absence of bran and other fibers in our food is one of the primary causes of constipation, as well as of cancer of the colon, diverticulitis, and hiatal hernia. Fiber and roughage reduce the transit time from food consumption to elimination, thus keeping the colon clean of undigested food. Soft, fiberless foods that lie for days and often *weeks* in your lower intestine and colon become prime breeding places for cancerous cells to colonize. The longer the passage time, the greater the risk of tumor development.

Among certain "uncivilized" peoples whose diet is high in fiber, the transit time is eight to twelve hours for children and fourteen to eighteen hours for adults. Among Westerners whose diets are virtually void of fiber, transit time ranges from three days to two weeks. Even though you eliminate every day, your transit time may be several days. No wonder there is so much cancer of the colon.

When the millers remove the wheat germ and bran from the wheat kernel, they also remove: 27 percent of the protein, 57 percent of the pantothenic acid (an essential amino acid), 60 percent of the calcium, 78 percent of the magnesium, 94 percent of the pyridoxine (Vitamin B-6), 66 percent of the riboflavin (Vitamin B-2), 74 percent of the potassium (necessary for muscle tone and nerves), 50 percent of the linoleic acid, 97 percent of the thiamine (Vitamin B-1), and 76 percent of the iron.

In addition, they extract significant amounts of phosphorus (necessary to build teeth and bones), manganese (necessary for reproduction and growth), sulfur, iodine (necessary for thyroid gland), fluorine, chloride, sodium, silicon, boron, inositol, folic acid (necessary for metabolism), choline (needed by the liver), and Vitamin E and copper (necessary for red blood cells).

This deadly refining process has occurred in all grains that are labeled refined, including white rice.

When I began to buy bread made from whole grain flour instead of refined flour, my youngest son rebelled. "I don't like that heavy brown bread," David said. "Please buy me that nice, soft white bread."

So for a time, I compromised and fed him molasses-sweetened squaw bread. Though this bread was still made with white flour, there was no refined sugar in it.

For much of his life, David had experienced chronic constipation. During one particularly difficult bout, he asked us to recommend a laxative.

Bob told him, "David, you don't need a laxative. The best thing you can do is take a couple of tablespoons of unprocessed bran every day, then start eating whole grain bread like the rest of us."

David made a face, but took the suggestion. His life-long constipation soon ceased to exist.

At the time of this writing, David is in Israel studying. During his first week there, he wrote home, "The bread at school is terrible! It's that gooey white stuff I used to love. I'd rather go without than eat it."

David's eating habits were observed by others at the Israeli school, including the student-faculty cooks of the institution. One day the chief steward asked him, "How would you like to come in the kitchen any night—any time, in fact—and bake anything you'd like?"

"Do you have whole grain wheat flour?" David asked.

"No, but we'll get it for you."

David began baking his own bread and sharing it with others. That started a chain reaction that has since resulted in a choice of bread being available in the dining hall: dead bread, baked from bleached white flour, and living bread, made from whole grain flour.

Observing God's physical blessings on David's body, many others in the school have gradually swung over to a better way of eating.

Three years ago, David's body evidenced the cumulative effect of sowing malnutrition. Today it shows the positive effect of sowing proper nutrition.

Caffeine Beverages. Coffee, tea, and cola drinks all contain large amounts of caffeine, as do chocolate and certain medications. And caffeine is a drug. Verner Stillner, M.D., M.P.H., in an interview for *Prevention* magazine, declared caffeine to be "the most utilized and abused drug."

Concerning the use of this drug, the American Pharmaceutical Association's *Handbook of Nonprescription Drugs* (5th edition, 1977) says, "Doses larger than 250 milligrams often cause insomnia, restlessness, irritability, nervousness, tremor, headaches, and in rare cases, a mild form of delirium manifested as perceived noises and flashes of light."

It takes just *two cups* of strong, black coffee or tea to deliver 300 milligrams of caffeine. In comparison, a twelve-ounce can of Coca-Cola contains 64.7 milligrams of caffeine; a can of Pepsi, 43.1 milligrams; an Excedrin tablet, 64.8 milligrams; a No-Doz, 100 milligrams; and a capful of Bromo-Seltzer, 32.5 milligrams. A Vivarin capsule packs a 200-milligram wallop!

Drinking coffee is such an all-American habit that those who refrain from imbibing the beverage stand out like the proverbial sore thumb. Recently, while I was at lunch with some friends, the waitress poured coffee for us all without asking if we wanted it.

"I'm sorry," I told her, "but I don't drink coffee."

She graciously accepted my refusal. But one of the ladies laughed. "I know coffee's not supposed to be good for you," she said. "But I just pray over it. That sanctifies it and takes the poison out of it. That's what the Bible says to do."

I knew she was referring to Jesus' words in Mark 16:18, ". . . if they drink any deadly thing, it shall not hurt them," and Paul's words to Timothy, "For everything created by God is good, and nothing is to be rejected, if it is received with gratitude; for it is sanctified by means of the word of God and prayer" (1 Tim. 4:4, 5, NASB).

Both of these Scriptures are frequently quoted to me and members of my family when we decline caffeine-laden drinks and certain foods. They are often used in defense of ingesting anything a person desires to eat or drink on the presumptions that: (1) drinking deadly things won't hurt the believer, and (2) praying over harmful food or drink will render it harmless.

Nowhere does the Bible indicate that one is knowingly to take poison or any harmful substance into his body, trusting God to detoxify it. Was Jesus supposed to obey Satan's challenge to cast himself down from the pinnacle of the Temple, trusting the angels to catch him? Both actions fall under the category of "testing God," a practice God decried in Deuteronomy 6:16, "Ye shall not tempt the Lord your God."

Satan tempts believers to misuse their bodies and prevail upon God to deliver them, just as he tempted Jesus to act irresponsibly and invoke God's power to save him. But as Jesus saw through Satan's trickery, we also must see through his thinly veiled attempts to lead us to harm.

God has much to say about the right treatment of our bodies. He plainly tells us that our bodies are the temples of the living God (1 Cor. 6:19; 2 Cor. 6:16), and that if anyone harms these temples, God will destroy him (1 Cor. 3:17). This is no lightly given statement, and we must reckon with it.

People are prone to think, "But I have eaten or drunk such and such for this amount of time, and it hasn't bothered me yet. Therefore, it won't affect me in the future." This kind of thinking can bring terrible harm to one's body because the Scriptures declare,

"Be not deceived; God is not mocked: for whatsoever a man soweth, that shall he also reap" (Gal. 6:7).

Today's Christians, in exercise of their liberty in Christ, have often quoted Mark 16:18 and 1 Timothy 4:4 as adequate justification for eating or drinking anything with impunity. The result? A generation of Christians who are suffering from countless physical ailments directly traceable to the foods they eat and drink.

BIBLICAL DIETARY LAWS

Though Acts 15:28, 29 indicate that most of God's dietary laws for the Jews are not required of the Gentiles, biblical laws relating to food have been scientifically proven to be the most healthy way to prepare and eat food. Those who have chosen to adopt these laws are finding themselves free from many of the illnesses that inflict mankind today.

One of these people, Burgess Parks, was spared from a horrible cancer-induced death simply by turning to the healing power that's available to us all through the intake of proper foods.

Burgess Parks was stricken with cancer of the colon in June of 1977, after which he underwent four major surgeries. As the result of multiple complications, he lay near death for several months. Through his strong determination and the mercy of God, Burgess lived.

A few weeks after his last surgery, Burgess and his wife, Mary June, embarked upon a study of nutrition, using the Bible as their textbook and the Holy Spirit as their teacher. Then they began eating only the foods that the Bible names as being good, excluding those that were processed or laced with chemicals. As a result, not only did Burgess lick his cancer and arthritis, but both he and his wife improved their eyesight!

Mary June says, "Our skin, hair, and nails are an indication of good health, and our general well-being is noticed by all our friends." (The Parks' books, which advocate the natural, nutritional approach to health, may be obtained by writing Parks Publishers, 315 Leawood Drive, Frankfort, KY 40601.)

It's impossible to give all the information needed to promote a healthy life in one chapter—or in one book, for that matter. I haven't even touched on regular exercise, which is also vital to building and maintaining a strong body. Numerous books are available that will help both you and your child set up a regular program of exercise.

Regardless of the area of health, we can always be sure to reap what we sow in our daily habits.

BIBLIOGRAPHY

Bricklin, Mark. *The Practical Encyclopedia of Natural Healing.* Emmaus, Pa.: Rodale Press, 1976.

Cameron, Ewan and Pauling, Linus. *Cancer and Vitamin C.* New York: Warner Books, 1981.

Dufty, William. *Sugar Blues.* New York: Warner Books, 1976.

Gerras, Charles, ed. *The Complete Book of Vitamins.* Emmaus, Pa.: Rodale Press, 1977.

Kadahs, Joseph M. *Encyclopedia of Fruits, Vegetables, Nuts and Seeds for Healthful Living.* Englewood Cliffs, N.J.: Prentice-Hall, 1973.

Rodale, Robert, ed. *Prevention.* Emmaus, Pa.: Rodale Press.

Scharffenberg, J. A. *Sweet Talk.* Arroyo Grande, Calif.: Concerned Communications, 1978. (Available for $2.95 plus fifty cents for mailing charges by writing P.O. Box 700, 146 Traffic Way, Arroyo Grande, CA 93420.)

Shannon, Ira L. *Brand Name Guide to Sugar.* Chicago: Nelson-Hall, 1977.

9: SOWING AFTER FAILURE

Cranston Timmons, an insurance executive, visited his elderly father "back home" on the farm. The amenities behind them, the two men sat on the large porch overlooking the well-kept fields. Sighing deeply, Cranston settled himself in his chair.

His father asked, "What's the matter, son?"

"Well," Cranston began, "several things. . . ."

"Such as?"

"Things are a little tense at home. . . . Janice is doing poorly in school . . . and, well, the business is growing so fast that it seems I've lost touch with the men."

The old man rocked in silence for a while. Then he said, "Looks to me like you've got two problems."

"Two problems?"

"Yes. The first one's crop failure. And the second one's your desire for a different harvest."

Cranston sighed again. "I guess you're right. But it's kind of late now for either one."

The old man laid his hand on his son's shoulder. "Not really. All you've got to do is plant again."

"Plant again? What do you mean?"

The older Timmons pointed. "See that field out there? What was growing there when you were a boy?"

"Just some scraggly corn. And a lot of stones."

"That's right. It was full of stones. When I bought this farm, the soil in that field was worn out from years of neglect. It was literally burned out. It was so bad, I couldn't grow anything there."

Cranston said, "But it's beautiful now!"

"Yes, but it took me literally months and months— even years—of hauling out debris. Fertilizing. Building up the soil. Then planting again and again. And now the crop on that field is a showcase. One of the best in the county."

The old man paused, admiring the field. Then he turned and pointed in a different direction. "What do you remember about that field? What grew there?"

"Soybeans, as I recall."

"And what do you see now?"

"Dad, I believe I'm looking at one of the finest blueberry patches in the state."

"You're right."

Cranston scratched his head in bewilderment. "But the soybeans did very well, didn't they? Then why did you change?"

"The soybeans were an excellent money crop. But I just didn't enjoy that kind of a harvest. I wanted a crop that would bring me in touch with the people. So . . . ," the old man smiled with pleasure at the thought, "I plowed up the soybeans and planted another crop, this time with different seed."

The old man looked directly at his son. "Remember, Cranston, every harvest is seasonal. Never forget that. You always have the opportunity to plant again."

PLANT AGAIN

Each of us is continually reaping a harvest that we have already sown. We're pleased with some of our fruits, bitterly disappointed with others.

If you are now reaping the results of a wrong sowing or poor seed, don't give up. Plant again! Undesirable harvests do not need to continue. In cooperation with the Word and the Spirit of God, you can predetermine a new outcome by the seeds you presently plant.

One of the most heartbreaking testimonials I hear from parents across the country is the guilt-laden admission, "My child didn't turn out very well. . . ."

I continually remind these parents that guilt does not come from God, but from the devil. Guilt binds us. God's love frees us. Guilt condemns us, but the Word of God tells us, "For God sent not his Son into the world to condemn the world; but that the world through him might be saved" (John 3:17).

If you are shouldering a load of guilt concerning one of your children, you might feel there's no hope for a new harvest in your child's life. Don't accept that feeling, because God says *there is hope.* God's Genesis Principle, his laws of sowing and reaping, do not bring despair. They bring responsibility—the responsibility to plant again.

Dr. Kantor is an administrator in a Christian college, a position he accepted after pastoring several churches during his children's growing-up years. He and his wife grieved over the fact that their oldest son, now an adult, had strayed from God.

But after months of semi-despondency over their son's wayward condition, they made a bold statement to God. "We will no longer accept the guilt for Grady's failure to follow you. Guilt would signal defeat. Instead, we will plant fresh seeds of your love in Grady's life. We will keep on planting and expecting an abundant harvest."

A few more years passed, and then they received the telephone call that brought joy to their hearts. "Dad, Mom, your prayers have been answered!" *The new harvest had come.*

Cynthia is one of the college-career young women who frequently attends our Bible studies. One evening she came to me with a troubled look on her face. "You said God forgives us when we ask him, didn't you?"

"Of course, he always does."

"Well, I was having this problem with a fellow," she began. "And, well, something went wrong, so we broke up. I asked God to forgive me for all my wrong words and actions, and I believed he did."

"Then what's the question?" I asked.

"Well, if God forgave me, why didn't he make everything all right?"

Cynthia's question is a logical one, one that needs to be addressed. The answer is this: God *does* forgive us for sowing a poor crop, but his irrevocable Genesis Principle is still in operation. A crop was planted. And a harvest will spring from that planting. However, today's harvest *will pass,* and tomorrow's *will* bring new fruits from the seeds you are now planting.

ASK FOR LABORERS

If your children are grown or living far from home, ask the Lord of the harvest to send other laborers to help plant new seeds in their lives. Sowing is never an individual affair anyway; you always will need laborers to help you. Pray that these laborers would go forth on your behalf, "bearing precious seed" (Ps. 126:6).

Bob and I often petition God to dispatch laborers to specific people to meet their specific needs. We are praying within God's plan when we do so, because God desires all people to be saved and delivered from bondage. And he uses his laborers to help set the captives free.

Laborers were sent into Glen's life. Though he had been raised in a Christian home, Glen stubbornly turned his back upon God for many years. Finally, long after both of his parents had died, his life was impacted by laborers who had been dispatched by his parents' prayers.

Today, a transformed Glen is himself a laborer, reaching others in the same way he was reached. He has set up and administers a twenty-four-hour "dial-for-help" telephone service. By his service, Glen pays tribute to those many laborers who shared the life of Christ with him—all in response to his parents' faithful prayers.

DEVELOP A HARVEST MENTALITY

Early in the book, I recommended that parents develop a sowing mentality, an awareness that everything they do or don't do is a seed. Equally important is a harvest mentality.

Be on the lookout for a new harvest, even if it's a small one. Think of the farmer who rejoices in the tiniest sprouting, encouraged with a spirit of expectancy. It will help you to count even the smallest blessing—even the most miniscule ray of light—as a harvest. Enjoy that single moment of response from your child.

It may also help you to think of other good harvests you have had: An answer to an urgent prayer. Deliverance from a moment of fear. The healing of a ruptured relationship.

All of these remembrances will contribute to the growth of your harvest mentality.

Remember the old, but meaningful, hymn: "Count your blessings, name them one by one, and it will surprise you what the Lord hath done." We will not be surprised as often by the Lord's blessings when we learn to develop our harvest mentality.

Al was excited about spending the summer with his cousin who lived on a farm. Rick had been born and raised on the farm, but for Al, a visit to the farm was a special treat. Both boys wanted to earn some money, so Rick's father told them, "You can use that plot of ground over there. . . ."

"What for?" Al asked.

"To plant a garden. Then you can sell the vegetables for spending money."

The two boys agreed, plowed the land, and planted the seed. Every day they watered and hoed. And every day they watched for the seeds to sprout. About a week after they'd planted their seeds, they were working out in the hot sun.

Al said, "Rick, there must be something wrong with this seed. It's not growing."

"Sure it is, Al. Just give it time."

"It's had *plenty* of time!" Al said. "I'm going to check it out."

And before his cousin could stop him, he dug up part of a row of corn and exposed the seeds. With a triumphant gleam in his eye he showed the seed to Rick. "See. I told you nothing was happening. . . . It's no use slaving out in this hot sun like this when nothing's going to grow here. I'm going to quit."

He threw down his hoe. "Wait, Al," Rick said. "Listen to me. Let me tell you something."

Al shrugged. "Go ahead. What've you got to say?"

Rick led his city cousin over to a shady place and the two of them sat down. "Al, I know it's hot. And I know we've worked out here for several days. . . ."

"Right on every count," Al commented dryly.

"But, Al, I've done this before. Several times. And, believe me, we're doing everything right. Within a few days, *the seeds will sprout.* They'll come up. They'll continue to grow. And if we don't quit we'll have a beautiful garden."

Young as he was, Rick had already developed a harvest mentality. He had planted before. He remembered that his faithful attendance to his planted seeds had produced a crop. By remembering these past harvests, he'd developed the patience to keep going in the present.

A harvest mentality is especially important when we are still reaping the fruits of yesterday's seeds.

Norris told me that he and his friend Kirk had watched what they ate for several months. "And what happened?" I asked.

"Nothing for me," he said dolefully, "but Kirk's skin began clearing up, and he had so much more energy. Why didn't the Genesis Principle work for me?"

Subsequent questioning revealed the facts: Norris had been a junk food addict for many years, whereas Kirk had eaten poorly for a very short time. Since Norris had sowed negatively for a longer period of time than Kirk, Norris's negative harvest lasted much longer than his friend's.

God's laws of sowing and reaping always work the same for everyone, but it is not always possible for you and me to know how long it will take to see a new harvest.

BE PREPARED TO RECEIVE

I have waited and waited—often impatiently—for many harvests: an answer to a question, the maturation of my faith, the development of my patience, the solution to a specific problem. And none of them came to me immediately.

As I prayed and waited, I didn't understand why I had not yet received a harvest from God, and I cried out, "Why?" I know now that I needed to be prepared to receive.

Some preparation comes through the passage of time, and some through diligent study of and obedience to God's Word. Other preparation occurs through prayer, both my prayers and those of others. If any one of these preparations does not take place in my life, then I won't receive.

Aunt Flora had willed an older, well-kept car to Chuck, who installed a front license plate that read "Tom." Tom was his teenage son. Naturally, as would any teenager, Tom was very eager to get behind the wheel of *his* car and drive it.

Chuck told his son, "When the time is right you can. The car's ready for you, but you're not yet ready for the car."

"Why not?"

"You aren't physically mature enough. And you have to be sixteen before you can get a driver's license, and...."

"And, what?"

"You've got to take driver's education and pass the exam."

You see, if Tom doesn't fulfill all the requirements, he won't receive the car. He hasn't prepared for the harvest.

When God says he will answer prayer speedily, he is speaking to the one who has prepared himself to receive. He can respond to your needs, desires, and longings only to the degree that you are ready to receive. I believe, in agreement with the totality of Scripture, that when Jesus said, "Knock and it shall be opened unto you" (Matt. 7:7), he was referring to prepared knockers.

KEEP SOWING

After I had taught a Bible study on God's Genesis Principle, Lois came to me and said, "Well, I planted a good seed last year: I gave one hundred dollars to the missionaries who came to our church. Now I'm just waiting for my hundred-fold return—to see if it really works—before I plant any more seeds."

Such an attitude has a wrong focus, because God said, "Cast thy bread upon the waters: for thou shalt find it after many days" (Eccles. 11:1). *Every time* you cast your bread upon the water, you will not receive an immediate return on the next wave. But as you cast and cast and cast—upon wave after wave after wave— the returns will begin coming to you as regularly as the ocean waves come into the shore.

She was just a little girl. And the day was very hot. She leaned on her shovel and looked across the huge garden plot. Here and there a few sickly perennials, spindly corn shocks, and gone-to-seed onions stood like beacons, trying to hold their heads high. Mostly the plot was covered by weeds.

She tried to push the shovel into the ground, but the hard crust resisted her weak efforts.

"I can't do it," she sighed. "The ground's too hard . . . the garden's too big . . . it's too late . . . and I'll never get finished."

Tears ran down her cheeks. "I wish I could do it," she sobbed, "but I just can't. I've tried and tried. But I can't do it . . . I just can't. . . ."

She didn't hear the footsteps in the weeds behind her. And she was startled when she felt a light touch upon her shoulder. Gentle fingers removed the shovel from her fingers. Her father's familiar voice said, "Let me help you."

He quickly spaded a small square of ground for her. "There," he said, "you can work on this little place. And when you've done this square, I'll help you again."

She went to work on the newly turned earth. The hot sun burned her face and arms. Her back hurt from the constant bending. Soon her fingers were dirt-encrusted and sore. But after a while she had planted the little square of ground, and she was ready for another.

Again came her kindly father. She marveled at his patience as he showed her how to turn the weed-infested soil, leaving another small square of soil for her to plant.

She planted again.

And with her father's help, she planted yet again.

After a while, she surveyed the expanse. To her delight, the many small squares of seedlings covered much of the plot that had looked so big when she started.

Suddenly she knew. "I can do it. Not all at once, but a little at a time. I get so tired sometimes. But I can do a little bit, then a little bit more. And one day my whole garden will be planted . . . a little bit at a time."

This story is true. Jehovah is the father. I am the girl.